USAF ILLUSTRATED

North American Aviation B-45/RB-45 Tornado

Kev Darling

Big Bird Aviation Publications

North American B-45 Tornado

A Big Bird Aviation Publication
First published in 2009

The right of **Kev Darling** and **Big Bird Aviation** to be identified as the author and originator of this work has been asserted in accordance with sections 77 and 78 of the Copyright Designs and Patents Act 1988 and International Treaties.

This book is sold subject to the condition that it shall not, by way of trade or otherwise , be lent, re-sold, hired out or otherwise circulated in any form of binding or cover other than that in which it is published and without a similar condition including this condition being imposed on the subsequent purchaser.

www.bigbirdaviation.co.uk

ISBN: 978-0-9559840-2-0

1	Chapter 1	A Bomber without a Role
17	Chapter 2	The Nuclear Tornado
25	Chapter 3	The B-45 Described
57	Chapter 4	The RB-45C Described
71	Chapter 5	B-45 Operations and Deployments
85	Chapter 1	RB-45C Operations and Deployments
103	Appendix 1	B-45/RB-45 Serials
107	Appendix 2	B-45C Solid Nose Modifications
110	Appendix 3	Technical Details

Also Available:

Cessna A-37 and T-37
Avro Vulcan Part 1
English Electric Lightning
Aircraft of the 8th AAF
Hawker Sea Fury

Showing clearly its B-25 and XB-28 roots this artists rendering of an XB-45 shows a turboprop aircraft.

NAA B-45/RB-45 TORNADO- CHAPTER ONE
A BOMBER WITHOUT A ROLE

With the final demise of Japanese resistance in 1945 the United States Army Air Force was faced with the dilemma of creating a new long range bomber force. Two of the primary machines, the Boeing B-17 Flying Fortress and the Consolidated B-24 Liberator, were already out of production and would be quickly removed from the front-line inventory. This left the Boeing B-29 Superfortress as the primary long range bomber although it was already obvious that the day of the piston powered military aircraft were passing, even so two final efforts were made to use this form of powerplant these being the Boeing B-50 and the Convair B-36.

The answer was the jet engine and the swept wing both of which came to the attention of the USAAF from intelligence gathered in Nazi Germany during 1943. While production of conventional aircraft continued unabated, Air Material Command instigated the development of new aircraft designs and the jet engines to power them, the latter were progressed under the aegis of General Electric with the programme designations of MX-414 and MX-702 that eventually appeared as the J35 and J47 respectively.

The airframe side of the equation began in 1944 when AMC contacted the primary aircraft manufacturers in the United States calling for designs utilising jet engines, and where possible swept wings with a weight between 80,000 and 200,000 lbs. Four manufacturers responded these being North American with the XB-45, Convair with the XB-46, Boeing with the XB-47 and Martin XB-48. Although all four would be offered development contracts it would be North American and Boeing who would succeed in producing aircraft that would enter operational service. The USAAF had intended to schedule a formal competition between the various contractors working on such projects, thus in 1946 the AAF decided to forgo the usual competition process. The selection process

Prior to any metal being cut North American Aviation produced various sized wind tunnel models. These were used to test various configurations before the design was finally set. This model ended up as an executive desk toy.

resulted in the Boeing and North American designs being chosen although by this time both were regarded as medium bombers. As requirements changed the B-47 remained as a medium bomber while the B-45 was redesignated as a light bomber.

North American's answer was the Model 130 that was covered by Contract letter AC-5126 that was issued to the company on 8 September 1944 that covered the construction of three prototypes designated XB-45. As design work progressed the contract was altered slightly so that the third machine became the YB-45, the tactical bomber prototype. In order that the B-45 could enter service within a reasonable time scale North American put forward a design that drew much of its inspiration from its previous wartime designs to which was added four jet engines, paired and carried in pods under the wings plus a bombing radar in the nose, although the wings showed much refinement utilising a NACA 66-215 aerofoil section at the root which tapered out to a NACA 66-212 section at the tip. On 2 August 1946 the AMC endorsed the immediate production of the B-45 this being followed by the negotiation and signature of Contract AC-15569 that called for an initial lot of 96 B-45A's ,North American Model N-147, plus a flying static test machine ,NA Model N-130, all for a fixed cost of $73.9 million.

On 17 March 1947, the first XB-45 undertook its maiden flight piloted by company test pilot George Krebs. During the one hour flight from Muroc Army Airfield, California, the aircraft was flown under stringent speed restrictions as the main landing gear doors would not close properly when the undercarriage was retracted. This problem might have been avoided by installing better landing gear uplocks however this time consuming installation was postponed as North American did not wish to delay the XB-45's flight. Even with this restriction the XB-45's performance was impressive. As a result of this successful first flight Air Materiel Command put forward an extensive test program for the three experimental airframes each was to be instrumented for a particular phase of the programme. The test programme was marred by the crash of the first aircraft, 45-59479, that killed two of the company test pilots. This accident was attributed to an engine explosion which caused damage to the tailplane that in turn caused structural failure of that section, as this was prior to the fitment of ejection seats the flight crew had no chance of escape. As might be expected, the crash of the first XB-45 resulted in a thorough investigation, the primary testing being undertaken in a wind tunnel that confirmed that the aircraft had insufficient tailplane area. The lack of ejection seats in these early machines had drastically reduced the pilot's chances of survival. In response ejection seats were installed in the other prototypes this would be followed by an advanced ejection system being developed for the forthcoming production aircraft. In addition future B-45's would be equipped with wind deflectors that were installed forward of the escape doors from which the other two crew members ,the bombardier- navigator and tail gunner, would have to bail out of in case of an emergency. The aircraft's tailplane area was also increased thus the span was increased from 36 feet to almost 43 feet.

Although the loss of the aircraft was tragic the flight testing of the remaining XB-45's continued. Pilots from the Air Force undertook minimal part in the initial flight tests during which they flew approximately 19 hours, while in contrast the contractors crews logged more than 165 flight hours on the two remaining aircraft during 131 flights after which the Air Force took delivery of the aircraft. The Air Force accepted the second XB-45 on 30 July 1948 this being followed by the YB-45 on 31 August. The acceptance of both aircraft were conditional as the cabin pressurisation and conditioning systems in both machines were incomplete although these deficiencies were rectified later.

Once North American had completed the installation of the pressurisation and conditioning systems of the XB-45's, further flight trials were undertaken by air force crews who flew a total of 181 hours in the remaining XB-45 between August 1948 and June 1949, when a landing accident damaged the aircraft beyond economical repair. The remaining YB-45 had limited testing value at that time due to an initial shortage of government furnished equipment. Even so the Air Force undertook a further 82 hours of flying time after which an air force flight test crew delivered the aircraft to Wright-Patterson AFB, Ohio, where the outstanding government furnished equipment was installed for bombing trials at Muroc AFB, California.

A craftsman puts together a large scale wind tunnel test model. This model features a remote system for controlling the flight control surfaces, also visible are the engine nacelle location marks on the upper wing.

Unfortunately due to excessive maintenance needs the YB-45 undertook only one test flight between 3 August and 18 November 1949 this being used to evaluate the long awaited government furnished components. At the completion of its systems and bombing trials the aircraft was used for high speed parachute drops that began in November 1949. These were completed by 15 May 1950 after which it was transferred to Air Training Command to serve as a ground trainer.

With the completion of the flight testing programme North American began production of the aircraft intended for service use. Even before the first Bombardment Wing was established doubts were being expressed as early as June 1948 following a meeting held in the office of General Hoyt S. Vandenberg, Air Force Chief of Staff who had assumed office on 30 April, the purpose on which was to ascertain the B-45's value to the air force and its future utilisation within the service. It was decided at that meeting that no further contracts beyond the initial one would be countenanced and that production would continue as planned up to the 119th airframe, and that the funds already made available for a further contract would be used for another purpose although this decision was later rescinded. A second contract ,AC-18000, had been issued in February 1947 which covered further production while a third contract W33-038-AC-21702 was placed in June 1948 although by this time the USAF had little desire for further aircraft, thus this tranche was later cancelled.

The use of the B-45 came under investigation by the Aircraft and Weapons Board who would hold a series

Seen soon after rollout is the XB-45 prototype being worked on by NAA flight test engineers. In this view the fighter type pilots canopy is clearly visible as is the original bombardiers troublesome glass covered nose section. Due to manufacturing problems many of the operational systems were missing from this aircraft.

Seen just prior to its maiden flight is XB-45 45-59479 sitting on the Inglewood flightline. This model had the shorter tailplane that would prove troublesome during early flight trials.

of conferences at which some board members suggesting that elimination of the co-pilot position and the AN/ARC 18 liaison set installed in that position plus the tail bumper that would reduce the aircraft's empty weight by 700 lbs. Also causing confusion was the attitude of the Air Staff who were under the

This raised view of the XB-45 shows clearly the anti glare areas painted forwards of the canopy and the inner faces of the engine nacelles. Also visible are the coverings outboard of the nacelles that reveals the outer wing panel attachment points.

Captured on an early test flight is the first XB-45. In this view the original bombardier glassed area has been replaced by a solid covering with the frames painted in. Also visible are the wingtip mounted pitot probes used to caliberate the aircrafts primary airspeed indication system.

impression that Tactical Air Command did not consider the B-45 suitable for bombing operations however Colonel William W. Momyer, who represented TAC at these conferences refuted this suggestion as this conclusion was probably based on previous studies by the command on the aircraft's excessive take off distances although North American and the engine manufacturers were working hard to counter this deficiency.

With its nose glass house restored the first prototype undergoes refuelling outside the flight preparation hangar. Also in this view is a fire engine just in case of an incident.

Seen just after touch down is 45-59479 landing at Muroc Dry Lake airfield. In this view the main undercarriage doors are still extended as they had a secondary role as drag inducers, they would be closed by the pilot just prior to engine shut-down.

This rear view of the XB-45 prototype shows the fairing over the rear gun turret position plus the location of the tail bumper. Also clearly visible is the gunners access door.

Another view of the XB-45 prototype complete with the solid nose canopy and extra wingtip pitot heads. This portrait was taken during the aircraft's early flight trials at Muroc.

In August 1948, 190 B-45's were tentatively contracted for production, however the programme's future was still uncertain. In order to justify the already issued contracts Headquarters USAF requested whether TAC required a bomber type a reconnaissance aircraft for long range duties and would a version of the B-45 fulfil their needs. The answer from Tactical Air Command was delivered quickly as they

With a Fordson tractor on one end of the towbar the XB-45 is towed out of its hangar for a days flying. By this time the proper three framed glass house has been installed although the extra pitot heads still remain.

With its gear down and locked 45-59479 poses for the camera. In this view the split bomb bays are clearly shown, note the difference in size.

did need reconnaissance aircraft although a reconnaissance version of the B-45 would not fulfil its requirements. The command also believed that USAF would gain greater knowledge of jet bomber operations by equipping two bomber wings with the B-45 in order to determine the tactics and limitations of the

Seen later in its test career is the XB-45 prototype. In this view the aircraft has been fitted with a tail gun turret although in this case the aircraft is undertaking JATO rocket testing complete with fire and thunder.

Another view of the JATO trials although by this time the undercarriage is retracting. The first to move is the nose gear which required less hydraulic fluid to move this being followed by the mains. Note all four flap sections are set in the take off position.

type. However the merits of these recommendations were academic as budgetary restrictions altered all future planning.

The axe that slashed the fiscal year 1949 defence expenditures did not leave the B-45 programme completely unscathed. The initial plan for the B-45

This underside view of 45-59479 clearly shows the the panel lines and the flight control surfaces. Note the different metal colours.

The two test pilots from North American pose for the camera at the forward entrance hatch during the flight test programme. Of note is the probe mounted through the pilots canopy.

Tornado force had called for five light bomb groups and three light tactical reconnaissance squadrons that were included in the USAF goal of seventy wings an unrealistic requirement for the period as the United States was in transition from a wartime footing to that of peace. Although the formation of the Soviet con-

This side on view of the XB-45 prototype shows the clean lines of the Tornado. The types main failing was the under powered engines.

trolled Eastern Block was giving rise to concern the reduced USAF programme dictated by continued financial restrictions being reinforced by President Truman's budget reductions for fiscal year 1950 . The reduced B-45 programme called for only one light bomb wing plus one night tactical reconnaissance squadron, although this meant that the procurement of aircraft had to be scaled down or that a substantial number of the aircraft would have to be placed in storage upon acceptance from the factory. Neither solution was appealing however the Aircraft and Weapons Board decided to cancel 51 of the 190 aircraft on order. The result was that $100 million would be released for other crucial programmes therefore only sufficient B-45's would be procured to equip one light bomb group, a single tactical reconnaissance squadron plus a much needed high speed tow target squadron. In addition there would be extra B-45's available to take care of attrition throughout the aircraft's service life.

Five light bomb wings were included in the seventy wing force planned by the Air Force however rejigging of the available forces to meet the reduced 48 wing target meant that the composition and deployment imposed by current funding limitations covered the formation of one light bomb wing. This wing would be allocated to the Far East Air Forces (FEAF) and would be fully equipped with B-45's. The equipment and training path chosen by USAF was to inactivate the 47th Wing at Barksdale and to replace the Douglas B-26's of FEAF's 3rd Light Bomb wing based at Yokota Air Base in Japan. Maintenance personnel of the 47th would also be transferred to Yokota so that FEAF would benefit from the B-45 knowledge gained by the aircraft's first recipient. The spanner in the works of this plan was that the B-45's could not carry sufficient fuel to fly to Hawaii, and equipping the aircraft with additional fuel tanks, a feature intended for later build B-45 models, was at the time impossible. The B-45A-1's powered by J35 engines had a ferry range of 2,120 miles and a take off weight of 86,341 lbs that included 5,800 gallons of internal fuel. Almost half of the fuel was contained in two 1,200 gallon bomb bay tanks and no additional fuel space was available. The following B-45-5's powered

Seen undergoing final construction are the second and third prototypes, just visible in right of this view is the already completed first aircraft.

Surrounded by various light aircraft is the first XB-45, at this point the aircraft still requires its anti glare paint applying to the nose and the nacelles.

by J47 engines had a similar take off weight and a negligible range increase of 30 nautical miles. As both versions were limited by range problems other solutions were investigated.

The first and only other possible alternative investigated was to move the required aircraft by sea however a minimum of ten feet or the entire outer wing panels would have to have been removed from each of the aircraft's wings, not a wise choice given the amount of work needed to re-assemble each aircraft. Other forms of other sea transportation were also investigated including using an aircraft carrier although all research into the transport question came to a halt as all were seen as unworkable. In early 1949, the Deputy Chief of Staff for Materiel Command stated that the overseas deployment of B-45's was currently out of the question for the time being as well as the immediate future. To begin with the B-45's were not fully operational as they had no fire control or bombing equipment and the aircraft lacked a suitable bomb sight although one was undergoing development. Structural weaknesses including cracked forging's in the primary structure had been uncovered in some of the few B-45's already flying. Until corrected these deficiencies precluded any deployment abroad. Air Materiel Command (AMC) also reported that the new J47 engine due to equip most of the B-45's was suffering from serious problems. The engine had to be inspected thoroughly after 7.5 hours of flying time. If they were found to be serviceable the aircraft could only be flown for an additional 7.5 hours before requiring a complete overhaul. Lack of funding prevented the purchase of sufficient spare engines to ensure that the B-45's could be kept flying if deployed overseas. AMC also anticipated difficulties in keeping those aircraft that remained in America flying even if they were close to the depots where the engines could be inspected and overhauled. AMC also postulated that the home based B-45's would need 900 spare engines to undertake a reasonable flying programme although none of these were available. Adding to the shortage problem was that North American F-86 Sabres had

The sort of take off test crews like to undertake when showing off, the low altitude, gear and flaps up spirited departure prior to dramatic power on climb.

first priority for the J47. The AMC report went onto say that the situation would be little altered until jet engines could be used for almost 100 hours between overhauls. This restriction meant that no jet aircraft could be stationed outside of America for at least another year.

It was not only the engines that were giving cause for concern, other systems installed the B-45 were also causing problems. Travelling at high speeds affected the Gyrosyn flux magnetic compass and the E-4 automatic pilot when the aircraft's bomb bay doors were open while the emergency braking system, served by the aircraft's main hydraulic system, was proving unreliable in operation. Also affected were the bomb racks whose mountings were poorly designed as the bomb shackles became unlocked during violent manoeuvres. The B-45's airspeed indicator was also proving inaccurate while the aircraft's fuel pressure gauges were both difficult to read due to needle flicker and were thus erratic. The powerplants were also posing a significant safety hazard as during start-up they often flamed out due to an imbalance in the fuel / air aspirator system that sometimes failed to work correctly. The temperature reading systems fitted to the engines jet pipes were incorrectly calibrated thus they failed to indicate the temperatures in the jet pipes while flying at high altitudes.

The aircraft's avionics were also causing serviceability problems in the early aircraft these centring around the AN/APQ-24 bombing and navigation radar system although few B-45's were fitted with this system. Malfunctioning of the pressurisation and conditioning system also limited the altitude at which the APQ-24's receiver and transmitter units could operate without failing due to overheating. Allied to this was the signal modulator unit that was not pressurised thus it to limited the APQ-24 capability. Additionally the mounting location of the radar scanner had an adverse affect on the coverage of targets especially when the aircraft was operating above an altitude of 40,000 feet. Coupled to the system unit problems were the ergonomics of the bombardier-navigators

The second XB-45 prototype, 45-59480, was similar to the first aircraft. In this view the bomb bay doors are open and reveal that the doors are constructed in two sections, the inner fitting inside the outer when fully open.

position as he had to attempt to manipulate two mileage control plots onto the radar screen although these were placed to the right and just behind his back. The layout of the B-45's radar system was no

This is the third Tornado prototype, 45-59481, seen sitting on the flight line with its main undercarriage doors down. Unlike the first prototype this machine featured the extended tailplane which improved the types stability.

This overview of the second prototype shows clearly the extended tailplane span. In common with the other prototypes the aircraft retains a fighter type pilots canopy and the three frame nose glazing.

better from a maintenance point of view. The USAF was still afflicted by a lack of sufficiently qualified personnel to maintain and repair the radar system thus it took up to eight hours just to remove and replace the APQ-24's modulator unit this being the system's primary troublesome unit. Adding to the dismal maintenance problem were shortages of spare parts, special tools, and ground handling equipment as well as engine hoists, power units, and engine stands.

The third prototype was used for numerous system trials prior to the B-45 entering service with USAF. In this view the aircraft has both its nose gear doors open plus the main gear doors.

B-45A 47-002 was the second production aircraft. It was retained for trials use, mainly at Wright- Patterson AFB.

NAA B-45/RB-45 TORNADO- CHAPTER TWO
THE NUCLEAR TORNADO

Prior to 1949 the USAF had never seriously considered the tactical employment of nuclear weapons apart from their use for strategic air warfare. Allied to this was the cost of these early nuclear weapons and given the difficulty in producing enough fissionable material they would remain few in number for many years. The change to this policy was the development and large quantity production of small tactical nuclear weapons thus the USAF earmarked such weapons again for strategic use only especially as warheads for proposed guided missiles. Although the Air Staff seemed happy with this strategy the Weapons Systems Evaluation Group conducted a study on the use of the nuclear weapon on tactical targets these including the effect of such a weapon on such targets as troops, aircraft, and ships massed for offensive operations plus naval bases, airfields, naval task forces, and heavily fortified positions. The study was concluded in November 1949 and found that tactical nuclear bombs would be effective on all targets. While it was as informal report, the Weapon Systems Evaluation Group's study was noted by the Air Staff although no action was taken until mid 1950, when the outbreak of the Korean War underlined the weakness of the North Atlantic Treaty Organisation forces should the Russians ever decide to seize the opportunity to attack Europe. This realisation forced events to move rapidly. Overall command and responsibility of these weapons would remain under the control of Strategic Air Command however the use of nuclear weapons would become Air Force wide.

In support of this policy change the Air Staff, on 14 November 1950, directed TAC to develop tactics and techniques for the utilisation of nuclear weapons in tactical air operations. Tactical Air Command had originally been part of the Continental Air Command when USAAF became USAF in 1948 although it gained major command status in December 1950. The directive received a further push in January 1951 when an Air Staff programme was outlined to ensure that TAC would become nuclear capable as soon as

Complete with large buzz numbers under the wings B-45A 47-011 undertakes a pre-delivery flight. The aircraft served with the 47th Bomb Wing before being retired for spares recovery purposes. Of note is the four digit tail number as used by all the operational aircraft.

possible. The B-45 would be at the forefront of the new plan as the aircraft also became the first light bomber fitted for nuclear weapons delivery. Turning the TAC nuclear capability into a reality would be difficult as the secrecy surrounding the production of the first weapons that created difficulties for both NAA and the AAF. Due to the dissemination of incorrect information the B-45 could not have been used as a nuclear weapons carrier without major internal modifications to the bomb as the main spar that travelled across the aircraft's bomb bay limited the size of weapon that could be carried. Making the task of Tactical Air Command more difficult was the decision to extend the use of nuclear weapons to all combat forces thus the B-45's acquired by TAC would no longer remain under direct control. This also meant that TAC would have too few aircraft to develop tactical operational techniques with the new weaponry. Further complications arose when the smaller, safer and lighter nuclear bombs entered the stockpile earlier than expected, again intensive secrecy had accompanied the new developments. These changes meant that the B-45 would be unable to carry any of the new bombs without first undergoing further extensive modification to carry these new weapons.

In December 1950 some sixty B-45's were earmarked for nuclear weapons delivery duty, this consisting of three squadrons of 16 aircraft each, plus 12 attrition machines. This total would be reduced to forty aircraft in mid 1951 although it was increased again in mid 1952, when fifteen other B 45's were added to the special modification programme. The Air Staff directed AMC to modify a first lot of nine aircraft to carry the small bombs for which designs were then available. This initial project would allow for suitability tests by the Special Weapons Command that was established in December 1949, this was later redesignated Air Force Special Weapons Center being assigned to Air Research and Development Command

The different metal colours of the B-45 are revealed in this overview of 47-011. Unlike later build machines this aircraft retained the fighter type canopy fitted to the prototypes plus the original three frame nose glazing.

in April 1952. However the diversion of these aircraft meant that TAC had less test aircraft to undertake its new tasks. To speed up the development programme five of the nine aircraft would be equipped with the AN/APQ-24 bombing and navigation system while the remaining four would be fitted with the AN/APN-3 Shoran navigation and bombing system, plus the visual Norden M9C bomb sight. North American would bring the nine aircraft up to the required special weapons configuration for a total cost of $512,000.

By mid 1951 the programme for operational use of the B-45 in possible nuclear operations was finally established. The aircraft involved in this programme were code named Backbreaker and included, in addition to the B-45 light bombers, 100 Republic F-84 Thunderjet fighter bombers. As the availability of modified B-45's increased the programmes status was accelerated thus it became second only to a concurrent and closely related modification program involving various SAC bombers. In August 1951 the programme received further impetus as the Air Staff confirmed that nuclear capable modified B-45's, equipment, and allied support would be supplied to enable units of the 47th Bombardment Wing in the United Kingdom to achieve a proposed operational nuclear capability by April 1952. In addition to the first batch of nine aircraft, the programme would be extended to cover a further 32 B-45's, the latter modification programmes cost being set at $4 million One B-45A was destroyed by fire in February 1952 and not replaced thus reducing the available total from 41 to 40 aircraft. Of the $4 million allocated to the project some of the funds were diverted from other Tactical Air Command projects that were later cancelled. The Air

Another view of an early production machine, this time 47-014. In this veiw the aircraft has its bomb bay doors fully open. Just visible is the fuel dump vent just aft of the tail bumper.

Staff requested that sixteen of the aircraft be ready by 15 February 1952 while the remainder should be available by 1 April.

The modifications applied to those airframes chosen for the Backbreaker programme were extensive. Equipment had to be installed in the aircraft for carry-

Never used by USAF this machine was used for experimental purposes for which it was designated EB-45A. Not often seen is the nose entrance ladder used by the pilots and the bombardier-navigator to enter the aircraft.

Prior to entering service with the 47th Bomb Group B-45A-NA-5 47-025 was used to clear the type for conventional weapons usage. Here clutches of 500 lbs bombs depart the rear bomb bay although some reports state that the type was unstable during bomb drops.

ing three different types of nuclear weapons which in turn necessitated some structural modifications to the bomb bay. Special carrying cradles were provided for each type of weapon while special hoisting equipment was required for loading each type into the Backbreaker B-45's. To support the delivery of each weapon a large amount of advanced electronics equipment had to be installed replacing the standard equipment while further modifications added new defensive systems and extra fuel tanks to the airframe. North American and the Air Materiel Command's San Bernardino Air Materiel Area, in San Bernardino, California, shared the modification responsibilities for the B-45 Backbreaker program. In early 1952 the nine B-45's, already modified to a limited Backbreaker configuration by AMC and North American were returned by TAC to San Bernardino for completion of the modifications, thus bringing them up to the same standard as the main tranche. Reworking of the other 32 B-45A's, later reduced by one after an accident, also took place at the San Bernardino Air Materiel Area during the first three months of 1952 with North American being responsible for furnishing all necessary modification kits. Fortunately good co-operation between the AMC, North American and equipment sub-contractors meant that the entire modification programme was completed without significant delays. Much of the electronic and support components required for the Backbreaker configuration were of a new and advanced designs and were in very short supply. The requirement for the AN/APQ-24 radar for the B-45 placed it in direct competition with Strategic Air Command programmes. As delivered the replacement radar's were not configured for the delivery of nuclear weapons thus those few available AN/APQ-24 sets had to be modified to the new configuration. SHORAN units were also in short supply thus a quantity had to be diverted from the Far East Air Force and Tactical Air Command's Douglas B-26 upgrade programme.

Other challenges facing those undertaking the Backbreaker programme centred around shortages of minor equipment items that were required to integrate some of the aircraft's systems. Some of the new equipment could not be installed before connectors were manufactured whilst other much needed components simply did not exist. One of the major omissions was the bomb scoring unit which consisted of a series of switches and relays that controlled the release of specific weapons in concert with the radar bombing system. As no such device existed each unit had to be manufactured at AMA San Bernardino. The Air Materiel Area also made parts for the A-6 chaff dispenser that including a removable chute for easier maintenance. North American also manufactured special fuel flow totalisers for the fuel system in order to control the rate and amount of fuel supplied to the engines, this unit also assisted in the supply of correct contents gauging to the crew whilst maintaining a balanced fuel feed. North American was also responsible for the manufacture of special equipment to integrate the AN/APG-30 radar with the rest of the Backbreaker B-45's tail defence system The Fletcher Aviation Corporation of Pasadena, California, was responsible for the production of the extra fuel tanks while AMC's Middletown Air Materiel Area in Middletown, Ohio manufactured the special slings that were required to carry some of the new weapons.

While the Backbreaker modifications were extensive the AMC and the manufacturers also had to cope with various existing engine problems which needed curing as the airframe modifications would be useless without them. A report by the General Electric Company field representative advising the 47th Bombardment Group throughout most of 1951 indicated that the J47's powering the Backbreaker aircraft would share some of the flaws of the types previous powerplants. The J47's available at that time suffered from turbine failures similar those that had afflicted the earlier Allison built J35's. Also subject to failure were the turbine tail cones that fractured when the J47 overheated. Flight stresses also caused oil leaks that meant that the engines had to be removed for repairs and ground test runs all of which required a lot of man-hours to rectify. While the USAF did not expect any new engine to be problem free from the outset the urgency surrounding the Backbreaker modification programme made these difficulties more significant.

In July 1952 the Air Force decided to increase the number of nuclear capable B-45 aircraft by a further

Seen lifting off under full power is B-45A 47-026 complete with a solid nose and a fully framed canopy. By this time the buzz number under the wing had been replaced by USAF titling.

B-45C Tornado 48-001 would never enter front line service with usaf being retained as a testbed by the manufacturers. The aircraft was lost in 1950 after suffering structural failure.

fifteen aircraft. The proposed configuration was that of the Backbreaker aircraft plus improvements based on experience and in service modifications. The primary updates covered the Backbreaker aircraft's tail defence system, the fuel flow totaliser that had been manufactured for the first 40 Backbreaker B-45's although they had not been installed due to production delays. Another important change required relocation of the carrier supports required by a specific type of nuclear weapon be moved into the forward bomb bay thus allowing for the installation of a 1,200 gallon fuel tank in the rear bay. The fitment of this extra fuel tank would give the aircraft an increase in range of approximately 300 nautical miles.

By September 1952 after a design conference with North American the USAF decided on the improved Backbreaker configuration and established a programme for procurement and installation of the necessary modification kits. The Air Force then allocated $2.2 million for modification of the fifteen additional B-45's plus a further $3 million for retrofit of the first 40 Backbreaker aircraft. The primary depot allocated to this task was the San Bernardino Air Materiel Area who would undertake the new modifications and would also be responsible for the provision of all necessary kits for the Backbreaker retrofit although these would be done in the field by unit engineers. Initially it was thought that the modification programme would proceed on time as it involved less work than the original Backbreaker modification. However the programme was subject to slippage as during the second half of 1952 the Air Materiel Command was in the process of transferring certain responsibilities from its headquarters to the various air materiel areas. This resulted in delays in processing engineering data and purchase requests this in turn delayed the manufacture of the field modification kits and their delivery by North American. Further difficulties occurred at North American as the contractor was no

Bailed to Northrop Aircraft as an EDB-45C 48-005 was used as a drone control test aircraft on behalf of USAF. Note the lack of wingtip tanks and the cone over the tail gun turret position.

longer tooled for constructing the B-45 and was working to capacity on other products. As a result of these deficiencies modification kit deliveries did not begin until July 1953 this pushing installation back four months. In September 1953 the USAF added a further three B-45's to the modification programme however as two of the original conversion batch aircraft had been retired and one had crashed the total still remained at fifteen. Completion of the conversion programme was delayed until March 1954 as later build machines were slotted into the programme to compensate for a lack of available B-45A's.

While the Backbreaker modifications and retrofit enabled the B-45's to handle several types of the smaller nuclear weapons, the modified aircraft were unable to carry and deliver the special weapons needed for the tactical interdiction mission thus in 1953 ,due to the increasing availability of nuclear weapons, the USAF thought of transferring this responsibility from SAC to TAC. In the event the situation remained unchanged as neither command had the type of aircraft available to carry out the task until the Douglas B-66 destroyer became available.

This head on view of an early build B-45 shows the dihedral applied to the tailplane, this was needed to clear the jet efflux.

NAA B-45/RB-45 TORNADO- CHAPTER THREE
THE B-45A/C DESCRIBED

The North American B-45A-1, A-5 and C models of the Tornado were described as land based four engined jet propelled bombers that were designed to operate at high speeds and at high altitudes. The aircraft was tasked with the tactical bombing of both land and sea targets. Should the B-45 be required to undertake longer range attacks extra fuel capacity could be installed in the bomb bay while the B-45C could be fitted with external wingtip tanks. The basic crew consisted of a pilot, co-pilot, who also acted as the radio operator, bombardier- navigator and the tail gunner. The two pilots were mounted on ejection seats while the other crew member bailed out through hatches in the nose and tail, both positions being provided with wind deflectors. The crews duties saw the pilot in the forward seat under the canopy having all the controls to hand to fly the aircraft while the co-pilot acted mainly as the radio operator although his position was equipped with basic flight controls, basic engine controls, elevator trim controls and the emergency braking system although no controls were provided for the fuel and hydraulic systems nor were controls provided for the undercarriage, flaps or the aileron and rudder trim tabs.

The fuselage of the B-45 was constructed in the three sections, the major section stretched from the pilots front bulkhead to the rear fin post , aft of which was the gunners compartment. This section consisted of seven primary frames this being supported by further, lighter, frames these being riveted to load bearing longerons and stringers all being covered by alloy skinning. Across the bomb bay was the main spar , there being secondary spars fore and aft. Forward of the pilots front bulkhead was a separate nose section that housed the bombardier- navigator under whom was carried the radar scanner. Over the upper section was extensive framing which carried the glazing that illuminated the compartment. Attached to the rear of the main fuselage was the final section which housed the gunners compartment and his weaponry. All crew areas were pressurised and fitted with air conditioning systems. Unlike earlier bombers access between the fore and aft compartments was only possible when the aircraft was depressurised, the bomb doors were shut and the bay was empty.

The wings were constructed around a primary main spar with secondary spars carried fore and aft. Wing

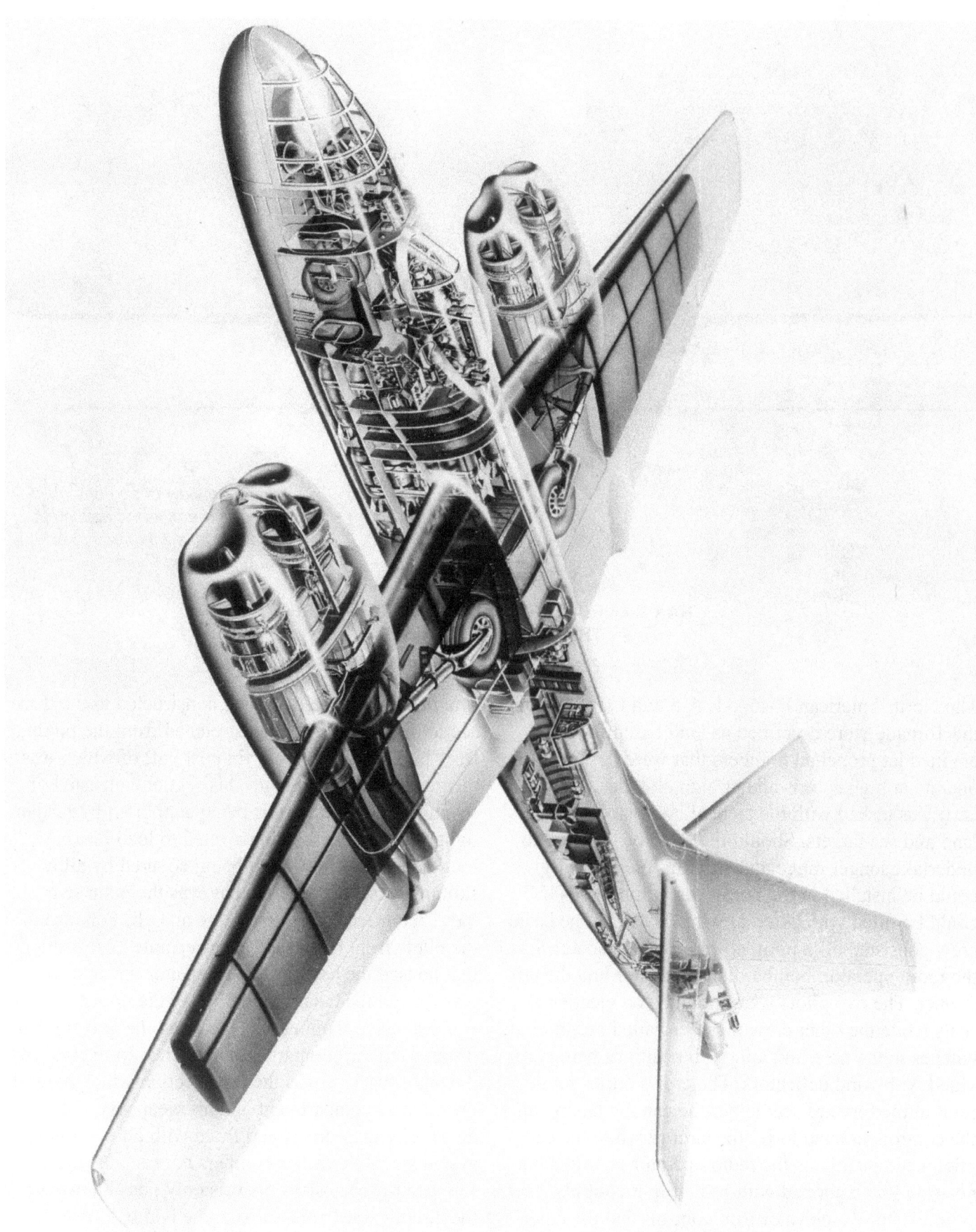

This cutaway provided by NAA to show the location of the aircraft's various components also reveals the position of the main wing spar which needed extensive modification during the Backbreaker modifications so that nuclear weapons could be carried.

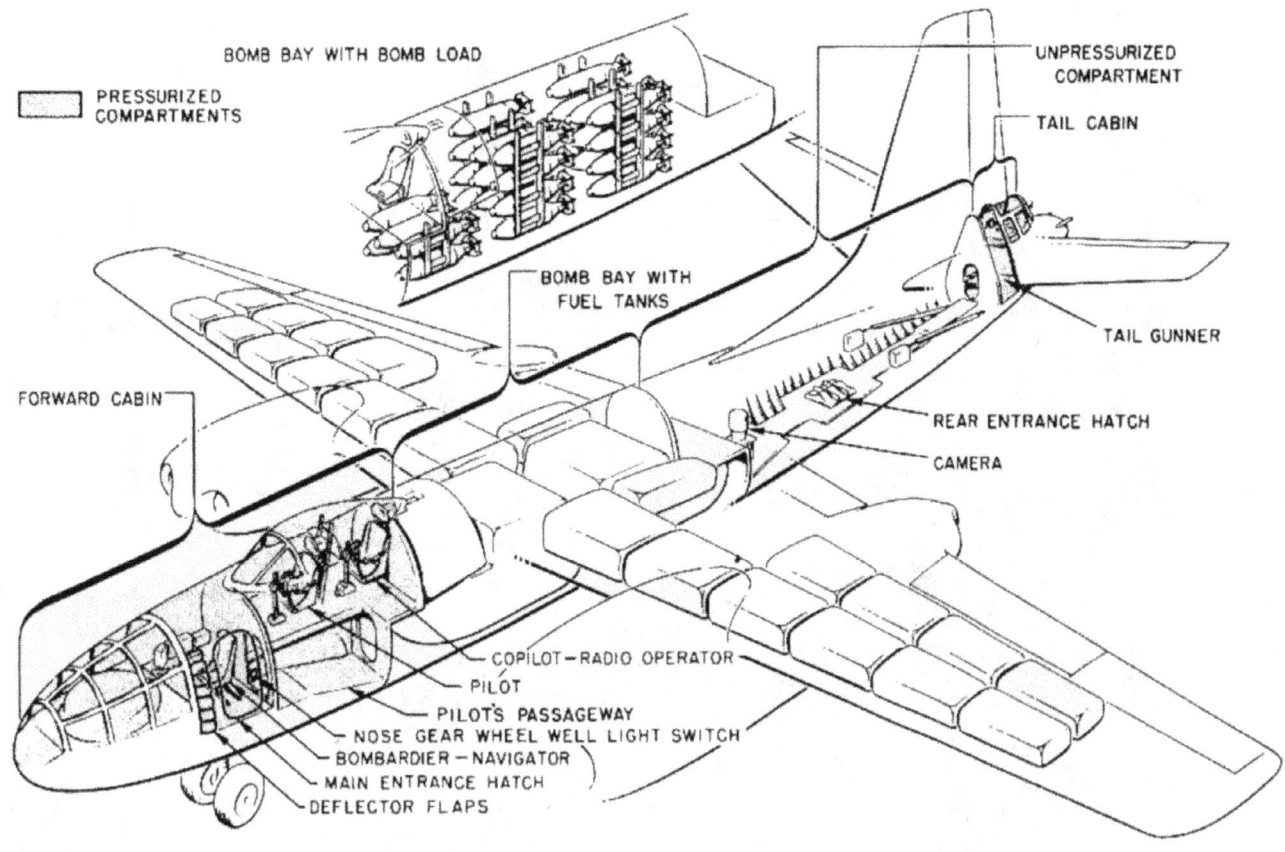

This diagram shows the crew locations, the main fuel tanks plus the alternate loads for the bomb bay including the bomb loads and the fuel tanks. Aft of the bomb bay is located the strike camera and the rear entrance hatch.

shape was provided by nose ribs, interspar ribs, many with cut-outs for the fuel tanks and stressed skinning overall. Extra strengthening was provided at the nacelle mountings for the engines and on the main spar at the main undercarriage mounting points. The wings were attached to the fuselage spar sections using bolts fitted both vertically and horizontally. On the wing trailing edge were carried the flap sections these being mounted either side of the engine nacelles while the outer section of the wing was the mounting point for the ailerons. The flap sections and ailerons were constructed around a single spar that had nose ribs forward and further ribs aft forming a distinct taper, all being alloy skinned. The tailplanes were of twin spar construction and were similar in construction to the wings, at their trailing edge were the elevators that were similar in construction to the ailerons. The fin and rudder were similar in construction to the other flight surfaces and all were fitted with trim tabs. The flight control surfaces were conventional in nature although all surfaces were fitted with hydraulic power boosters. The ailerons and elevators were controlled using a control wheel that incorporated a push to talk radio button, the auto pilot release, the nose wheel steering trigger switch and the elevator trim control switch. For access to the rudder pedals and other equipment the pilots control wheel column could be disengaged using a release catch. The co-pilots control wheel was similarly equipped with switches and could also be folded away as could the rudder pedals. To stop the control surfaces moving in an uncontrolled manner the flight control system was fitted with a locking unit in the cockpit although they could not be engaged while the hydraulic booster units were shut down. The trim tabs fitted to the flight control surfaces were electrically powered these being positioned using the single control stick mounted at the pilots position. The elevator and rudder boost was powered by a pair of electrically powered hydraulic pumps, both pumps were used to drive the

1. Fluorescent Light
2. Auto-pilot Power-off Indicator
3. Auto-pilot Trim Indicator
4. Radar Steering Meter°
5. Radio Compass
6. Flap Position Indicator
7. Landing Gear Indicators
8. Landing Gear Door Indicators
9. Engine Fire Detector Lights°°
10. Fire Detector System Test Switch°°
11. Fire Extinguisher Switch°°
12. Clock
13. Bomb Door Indicators°°
14. Bomb Release Indicator°
15. Accelerometer
16. ATO Indicators
17. Oxygen Pressure Gage
18. Oxygen Flow Indicator
19. Water Injection System Indicators§
20. Water Injection System Switch§
21. Remote-indicating Compass
22. Attitude Gyro
23. Tachometers
24. Rate-of-Climb Indicator
25. Exhaust Temperature Indicators
26. Hydraulic Fluid Level Indicator
27. Aileron Trim Indicator
28. Rudder Trim Indicator
29. Hydraulic Pressure Gage
30. Elevator Trim Indicator
31. Fuel Pressure Gages
32. Instruments Inoperative
33. Cabin Pressure Altimeter
34. Turn-and-Bank Indicator
35. Stand-by Compass Correction Card
36. Control Column Release Lever
37. Altimeter
38. Free Air Temperature Gage
39. Stand-by Compass
40. Elevator Trim Auxiliary Switch
41. Auto-pilot Release
42. Radio Microphone and Interphone Button
43. Nose Gear Steering Trigger Switch
44. Fuel Gages—Right Wing Tanks
45. Fuel Gages—Left Wing Tanks
46. Fuel Gages—Small Bomb Bay Tanks
47. Wing Tip Tanks "EMPTY" Indicators§
48. Fuel Filter De-icer Switch
49. Fuel Filter Ice Warning Indicator
50. Fuel Gage—Fuselage Tank
51. Fuel Gages—Large Bomb Bay Tanks
52. Oil Temperature Indicators§
53. Glide Path and Runway Localizer Indicator
54. Oil Pressure Gages
55. Pilot's Check List†
56. Marker Beacon Indicator
57. Airspeed Indicator

°B-45A Airplanes AF47-37, AF47-39 and subsequent
°°B-45A Airplanes
§B-45C Airplanes
†Located on top of instrument panel shroud on B-45A-1 Airplanes, and B-45A-5 Airplanes AF47-23 thru AF47-46

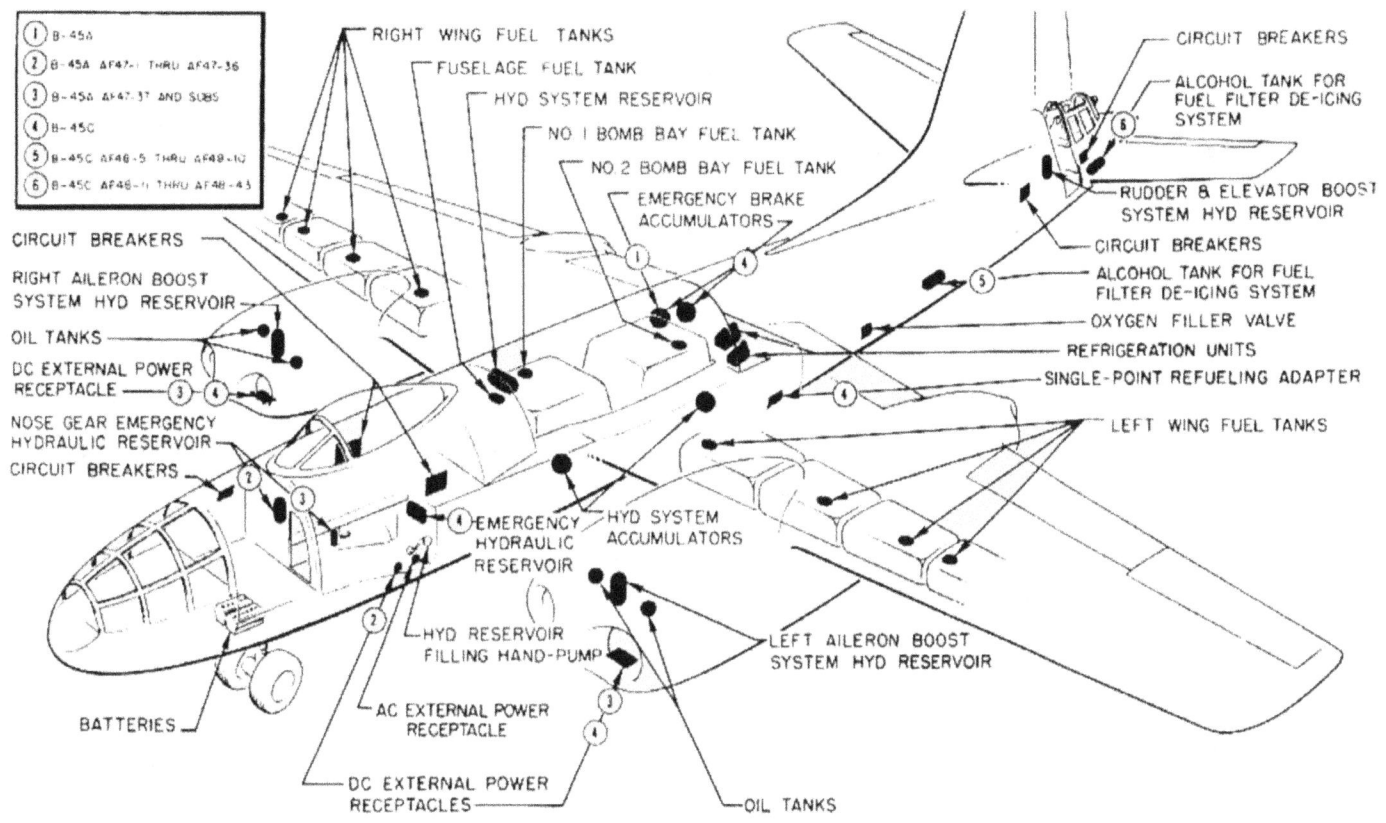

Shown in this diagram are the various serviceing points plus the differences between the various marques. Also shown are the main electrical and hydraulic components.

elevators while the rudder used only a single pump. In the first batch of aircraft low speed handling control was courtesy of a bungee this providing an elevator down force. In normal flight the bungee force was cancelled out by use of the trim tabs. In the B-45A-5 and the B-45C the low speed handling was managed by the downward cant of the jet pipes and spring tabs on the elevators. Instead of using electrically driven pumps the aileron boost system utilised pressure derived from the engine driven pumps powered by Nos.1 and 3 engines, however on the later build machines the hydraulic pumps from the other two engines were used to drive the surfaces. Aileron boost became effective as soon as the engines started however should any of the engines powering the aileron boost system undergo a power change or be shut down for any reason there was a corresponding increase in aileron forces. During normal flight enough hydraulic power was available to keep the aileron boost powered up when the engine was windmilling however once speed dropped to 140 mph or lower the bypass valve in the windmilling engine hydraulic system switched into the open position that made the system inoperative. When this happens the aileron forces become heavier as control became fully manual.

Also driven by the hydraulic system were the wing flaps that consisted of four sections these being located between the fuselage and the engine nacelles and between the nacelles and the ailerons. Available flap positions were selectable between fully up and fully down at forty degrees. Intermediate positions could be selected by the use of the selector lever in the pilots cockpit. Power for the flaps was supplied by the engine driven pumps. Emergency flap could be lowered using the emergency lowering system which diverted flow from the emergency pump to the flaps. Only the down selection was available using this system, no up selection was possible.

Hydraulics also powered the undercarriage system , the main undercarriage units retracted inwards towards the wing roots while the nose wheel assem-

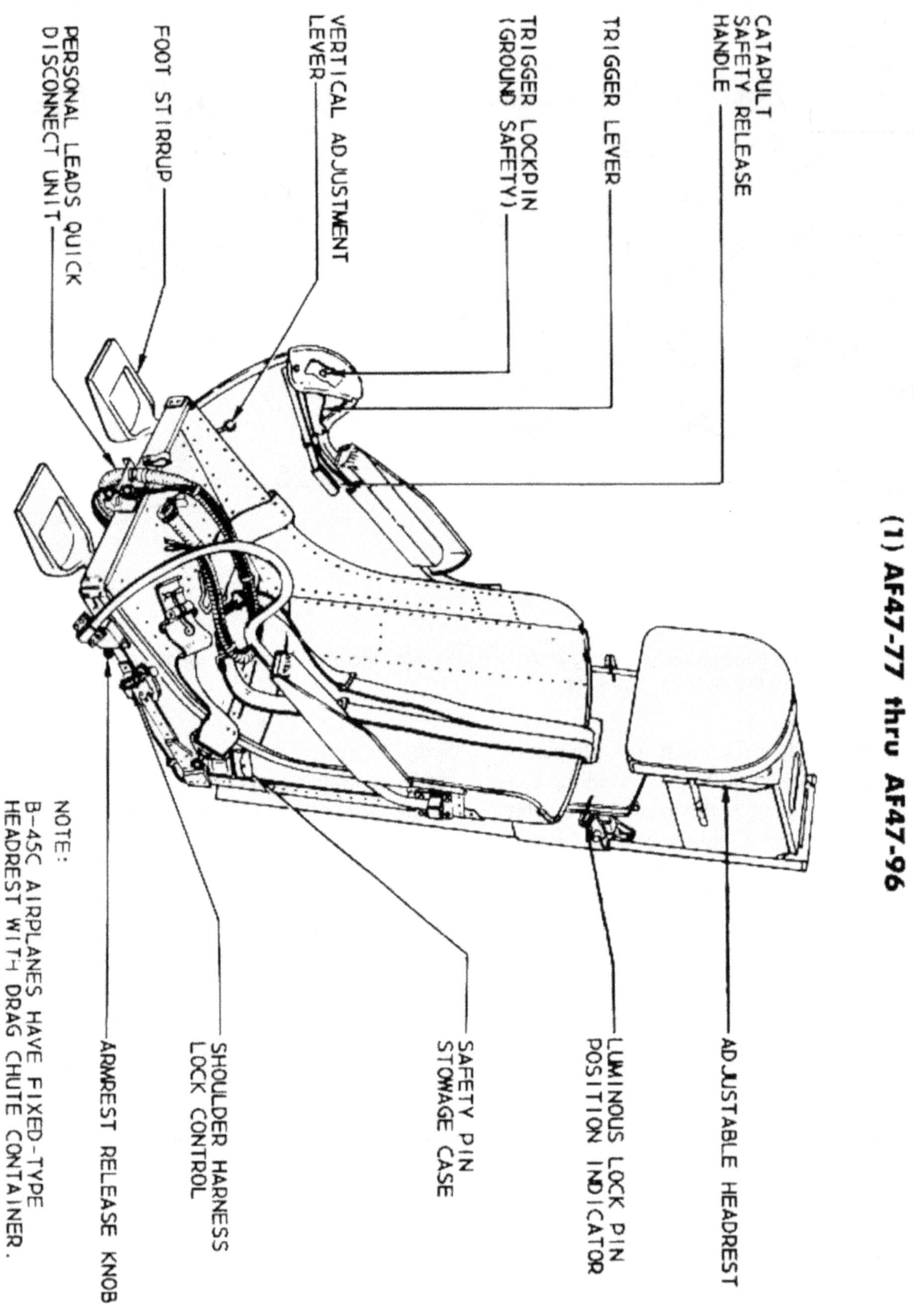

(1) AF47-77 thru AF47-96

Labels (clockwise around the seat diagram):
- CATAPULT SAFETY RELEASE HANDLE
- TRIGGER LEVER
- TRIGGER LOCKPIN (GROUND SAFETY)
- VERTICAL ADJUSTMENT LEVER
- FOOT STIRRUP
- PERSONAL LEADS QUICK DISCONNECT UNIT
- ARMREST RELEASE KNOB
- SHOULDER HARNESS LOCK CONTROL
- SAFETY PIN STOWAGE CASE
- LUMINOUS LOCK PIN POSITION INDICATOR
- ADJUSTABLE HEADREST

NOTE:
B-45C AIRPLANES HAVE FIXED-TYPE HEADREST WITH DRAG CHUTE CONTAINER.

The pilots flying the B-45 were lucky enough to be seated on ejection seats while the two other crew members had to bail out manually through hatches in the fuselage sides.

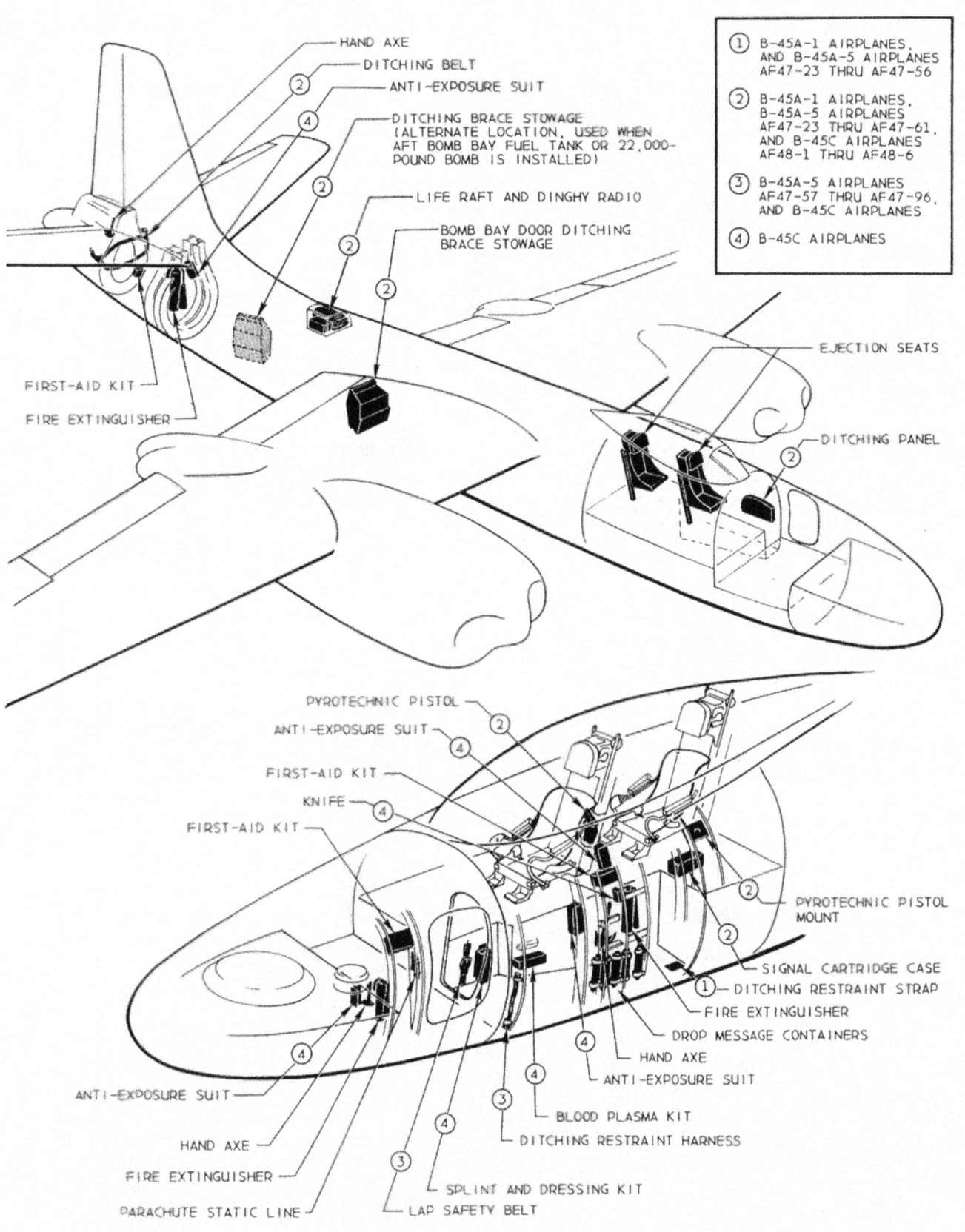

The B-45 was well equipped with emergency equipment that covered escape, ditching and survival.

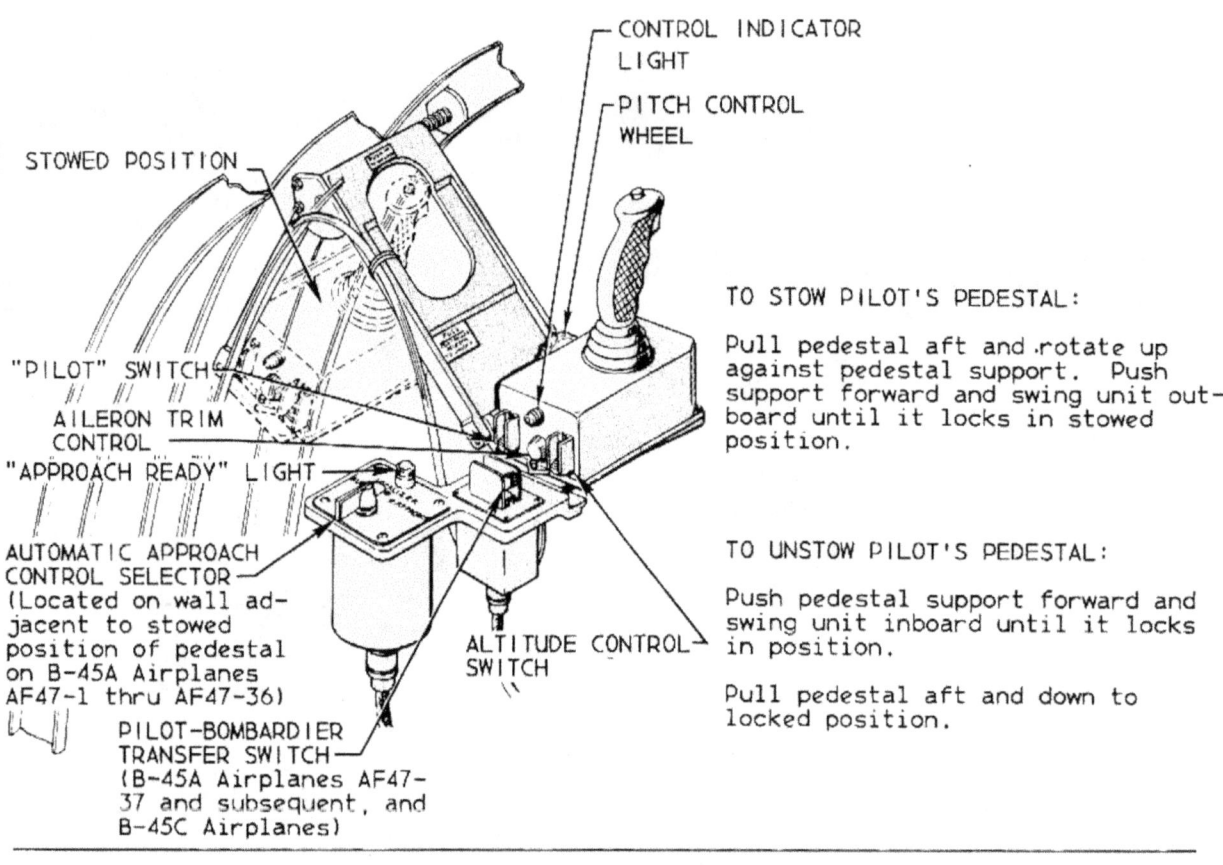

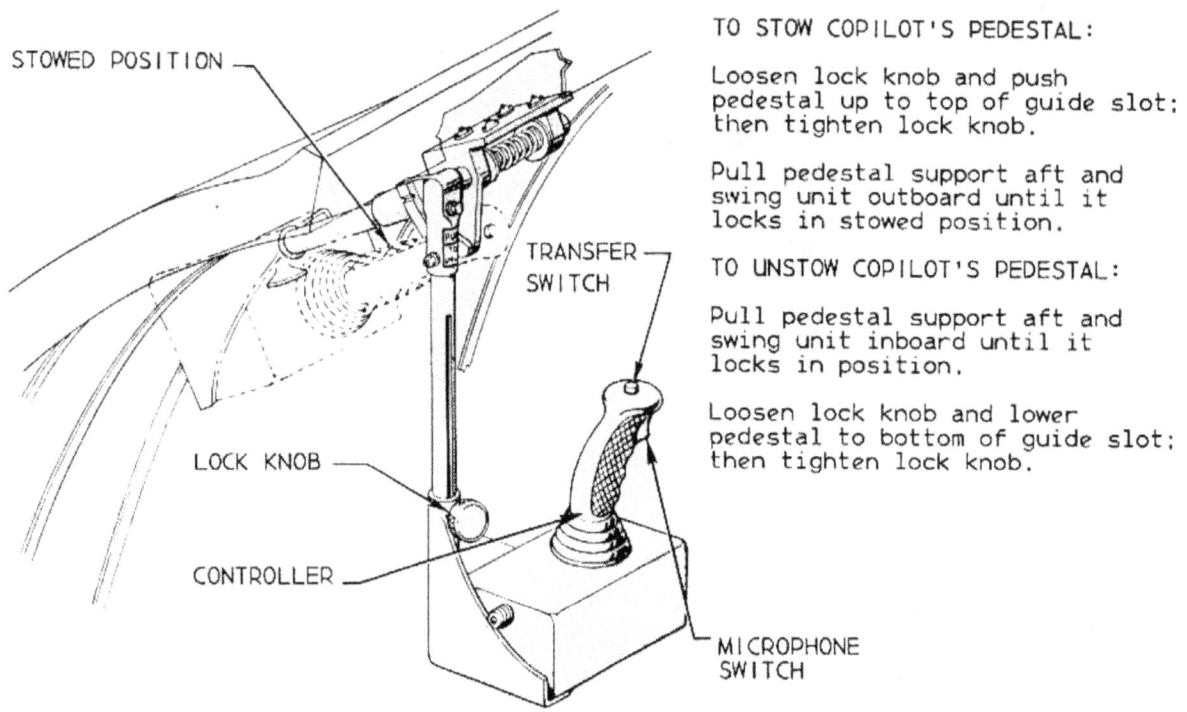

The pilot positions were equipped with a side stick controller for automatic flight control purposes. This could be stowed away when not in use plus the various marques that were fitted with this system.

1. Auto-pilot Release Button
2. Radio and Interphone Microphone Button
3. Elevator Trim Auxiliary Switch
4. Pyrotechnic Pistol*
5. Copilot's Check List
6. Auto-pilot Engaged—Power Off Indicator
7. Oxygen Flow Indicator
8. Airspeed Indicator
9. Turn-and-Bank Indicator
10. Attitude Gyro
11. Remote-indicating Compass
12. Rate-of-Climb Indicator
13. Fluorescent Light
14. Oxygen Pressure Indicator
15. Altimeter
16. Rudder Bars
17. Heat and Vent Floor Outlet

*B-45A-1 Airplanes, B-45A-5 Airplanes AF47-23 thru AF47-61, and B-45C Airplanes AF48-1 thru AF48-6

While the pilots position was equipped with controls for the entire aircraft the co-pilots cockpit featured less controls as his duties concerned communications rather than flying.

bly retracted aft into its bay. As the main gear retracted into the bays the wheel brakes came on automatically to stop the wheels spinning. The nose wheel unit also incorporated a steering unit which also acted as an anti shimmy unit when disengaged. The B-45 was also fitted with a hydraulically driven tail skid, this automatically extending and retracting in sequence with the undercarriage. During approach the main undercarriage fairing doors remained open to increase drag for deceleration during landing. Should the undercarriage selector be placed in the down position during landing the main gear doors will close auto-

This pedestal was mounted in the pilots position and covered engine, fuel and anti-icing management amongst other systems.

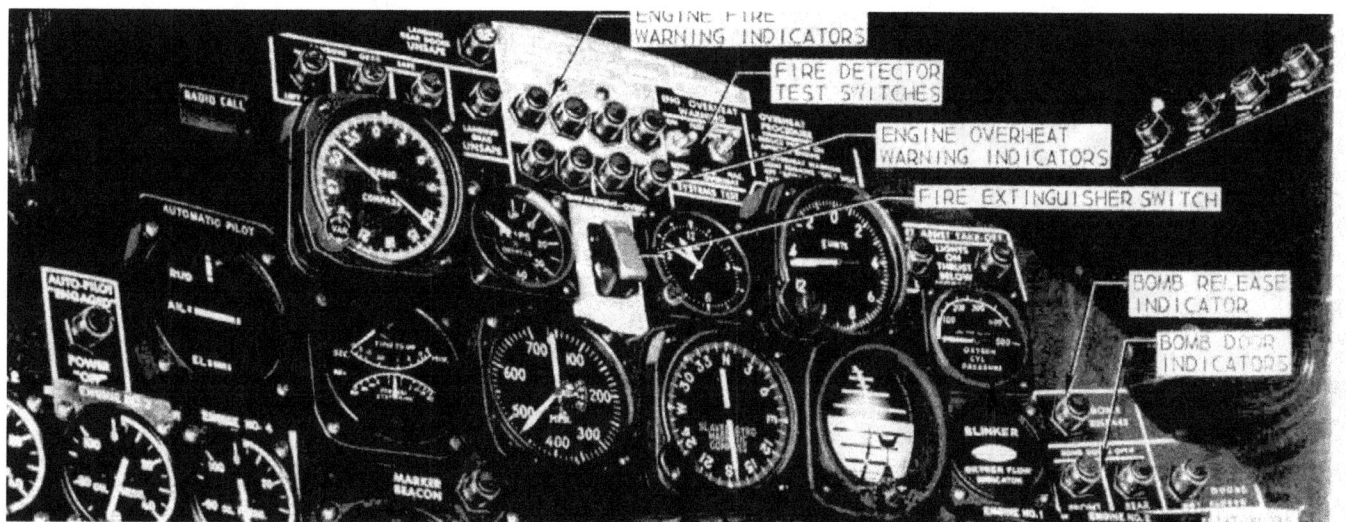
This diagram is of the upper panel fitted to the pilots position. It contained indicators for fire suppression, engine overheat warning lights plus the bomb release indicators.

matically on touchdown however should further drag be needed during the landing roll the selector had to be left in he neutral position although it had to be returned to down prior to engine shut down. In common with many aircraft the B-45 would normally be fitted with ground locks and a safety cover over the selector to prevent inadvertent retraction. Indication of the undercarriage position was courtesy of a light sequence thus green indicated fully down and locked, red indicated unlocked while amber indicated that the gear was in transit. Should there be a failure in the hydraulic system the undercarriage could be lowered using the emergency system. This was activated using a hand pump located behind the bombardiers position. The initial cycles released the undercarriage gear and door uplocks, after free falling the legs were pumped into the locked position. In the later built aircraft the hand pump was replaced by two switches located close to the forward bomb bay bulkhead in the rear of the pilots cockpit. Selection of door open and gear down will see the locks disconnected mechanically after which the undercarriage will drop down into the locked position.

Other hydraulic units driven by the aircraft's systems included the nose wheel steering unit which will only operated when the nose wheels are on the ground and the shock absorber jack was compressed. When operated by the pilot using the switch on the control wheel , this allowed the pilot to move the unit 45 degrees either side of the centreline. For ground movement the steering unit and anti shimmy unit could be disconnected by removing a pin thus ensuring these units were undamaged during ground movements. The aircraft's brakes were controlled using the toe pedals on the rudder pedals. For emergency use there were emergency levers at both pilots positions and that at the pilots position could be used as a parking brake.

The bomber versions of the B-45 were fitted with two different types of engines, the Dash One was powered by four Allison J35 engines mounted in pairs under each wing. Two variants were utilised these being the J35-A-9 and the J35-A-11. The subsequent Dash Five and B-45C were powered by either the J47-GE-7, 13 or the J47-GE-9, 15 all of which were manufactured by General Electric. Each Allison powerplant was provided with a pressure type oil system that contained 12.7 gallons of usable fluid. Monitoring of tank contents was via gauges mounted on the pilots panel. The oil system provided for the GE engines was similar in operation although the tank contents was reduced to 6.7 gallons of usable fluid.

To improve take off performance the B-45 could be fitted with external tanks mounted under the engine nacelles these containing water methanol. Injection of this mix into the engines could be used to improve take off performance. To use the water injection system the flaps had to be set to 20 degrees while the trim tabs had to be set at zero degrees.

The fuel system installed in the B-45 consisted of eight fuel tanks made up of 22 cells interconnected to make up the groups. Each wing group under normal circumstances fed the engines on that side of the air-

1. Fuel System Control Panel
2. Taxi Light Switch
3. Landing Light Switch
4. Code Selector
5. Navigation Light Switches
6. Formation Lights Switch
7. Fuselage Lights Switch
8. Fuselage Lights Indicator
9. Auto Code Switch
10. Emergency Alarm Switch
11. ATO Release Switch
12. ATO Ignite Switch
13. Surface Control Boost Switch
14. Engine Starters
15. Battery Switch
16. Horn Cutoff Switch—Landing Gear
17. Horn Cutoff Switch—Cabin Pressure
18. Bomb Door Switch

This panel mounted in the pilots position concerned itself mainly fuel management plus the controls for the JATO boosted rocket system. Other switches on this panel included warning horn cut-off switches and the bomb door switches.

craft although in an emergency a fuel system crossfeed line could be opened to supply fuel to the engines on the opposite wing. When the jettisonable wing tanks, each holding 1,250 US gallons, were installed they were referred to as No.4 fuel tank. Under normal circumstances each tank feeds the relevant pair of engines although should one become inoperative the remaining tank could be switched to feed all four engines. Unlike the main system the wingtip tanks had no gauging however each has an empty light that illuminated when the contents had been used. All fuel tanks were fitted with booster pumps as were the bomb bay tanks when fitted. When a single tank was fitted in the bomb bay both fuselage pumps were connected to the tank although when two tanks were installed only one pump is fitted to each tank. As these pumps have a greater output than the wing tank pumps the bomb bay tanks had to be used first. Should circumstances warrant it the bomb bay tanks and or bombs could be jettisoned using the

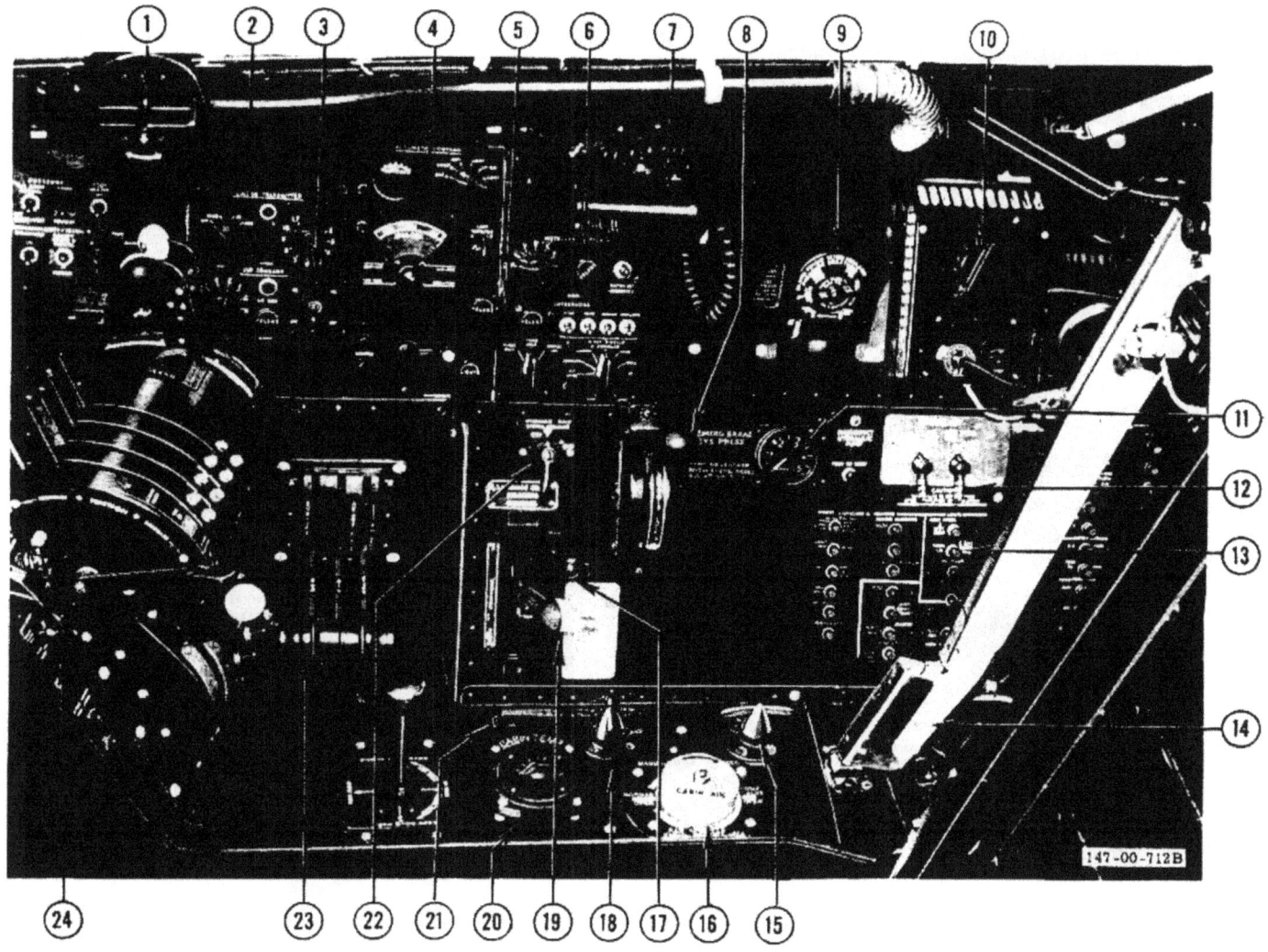

1. Heat and Vent Outlet
2. Liaison Transmitter Control Panel†
3. Command Radio Control Panel
4. Radio Compass Control Panel
5. Interphone and Mixer Switch Panel
6. Instrument Approach Control Panel
7. Fluorescent Light
8. Controls Lock
9. Oxygen Regulator
10. Heated Clothing Control Panel
11. Emergency Brake Hydraulic System Pressure Gage*
12. Emergency Hydraulic Selector Valves
13. Circuit Breaker Panels
14. Canopy Emergency Release
15. Life Raft Release
16. Cabin Air Valve
17. Landing Gear Lock Emergency Release
18. Wing Tip Tank Mechanical Release**
19. Landing Gear Selector Control
20. Cabin Temperature Rheostat
21. Cabin Temperature Manual Override Switch§
22. Hydraulic Main System Pressure Control Valve
23. Auto-pilot Engaging Handles
24. Bomb and Tank Salvo Selector Switch**

†B-45A-1 Airplanes, B-45A-5 Airplanes AF47-23 thru AF47-61, and B-45C Airplanes AF48-1 thru AF48-6
*B-45A-5 Airplanes AF47-77 thru AF47-96
**B-45C Airplanes
§B-45A-5 Airplanes AF47-47 thru AF47-96, and B-45C Airplanes

Other systems managed by the pilot included pressurisation and environmental switches, undercarriage controls, wingtip tank release and the auto pilot engagement handles.

salvo panel located at the pilots position. However there were proviso's to this instruction as the 310 US gallon tanks could not be jettisoned when the aft bomb bay shackles, Type D-7, for the 2,000 and 4,000 lbs bombs were fitted. The B-45 was also capable of carrying a 1,200 US gallon tank in the bomb

1. Heated Clothing Control Panel
2. Cockpit Light
3. Oxygen Regulator
4. Ammeters
5. Heat and Vent Outlet
6. Automatic Pilot Controller
7. A-C Voltmeter
8. Alternator Warning Light†
9. Alternator Switch†
10. Pyrotechnic Pistol Mount°°
11. Canopy Emergency Release
12. Canopy Defroster Outlets
13. Inverter Warning Lights†
14. Portable Oxygen Bottle
15. Inverter Switch†
16. Surface Control Boost Test Switches°
17. Disposal Container
18. D-C Voltmeter Selector
19. Main Hydraulic System Filler Hose
20. Landing Gear and Door Manual Emergency Controls§
21. Main Hydraulic Reservoir Filling Hand-pump
22. Bomb Door Manual Control
23. A-C Voltmeter Selector
24. Generator Overvoltage Lights
25. D-C Voltmeter
26. Circuit Breaker and Fuse Panel
27. Generator Switches
28. Signal Cartridge Case°°
29. Interphone Amplifier Auxiliary Gain Control
30. Alarm Bell

†B-45A-1 Airplanes, and B-45A-5 Airplanes AF47-23 thru AF47-76
°B-45A-5 Airplanes AF47-77 thru AF47-96 and B-45C Airplanes have three switches instead of four
§B-45A-5 Airplanes AF47-37 and subsequent
°°B-45A-1 Airplanes, B-45A-5 Airplanes AF47-23 thru AF47-61, and B-45C Airplanes AF48-1 thru AF48-6

While the co-pilot was supposed to be concerned with communications he also managed some of the electrical systems plus the landing gear emergency controls and the hydraulic hand pump.

bay although the pilot was warned not to open the bay doors as damage could occur to the tank although the pilot was allowed to open them when the tank was full or it required jettisoning. If fitted the wingtip tanks can also be jettisoned using the controls located at the pilots stations either by using a mechanical

1. Fluorescent Light
2. Emergency Brake Levers
3. Power Controls
4. Emergency Brake Boost Switch*
5. Radio Key
6. Liaison Transmitter†
7. Heat and Vent Outlet
8. Liaison Receiver†
9. Cockpit Light
10. Canopy Defroster Outlets
11. Interphone Panel
12. Radio Compass Receiver
13. IFF Control Panel†
14. IFF Indicator Lights†
15. Canopy Seal Pressure Regulator
16. Canopy Seal Pressure Gage
17. Radio Circuit Breakers
18. Liaison Transmitter Monitor Switch†

*B-45A-5 Airplanes AF47-77 thru AF47-96
†B-45A-1 Airplanes, B-45A-5 Airplanes AF47-23 thru AF47-61, and B-45C Airplanes AF48-1 thru AF48-6

The co-pilots left hand control panel was centred around the communication systems plus some of emergency controls.

release or the salvo panel. Refuelling the B-45 was through a single pressurised refuel point located on the left hand side of the fuselage, aft and below the trailing edge of the wing.

The B-45 electrical system fitted to the earlier build machines utilised four engine driven generators that supplied 28 volts dc to the aircraft which acted as combination generators and starter units. Once the

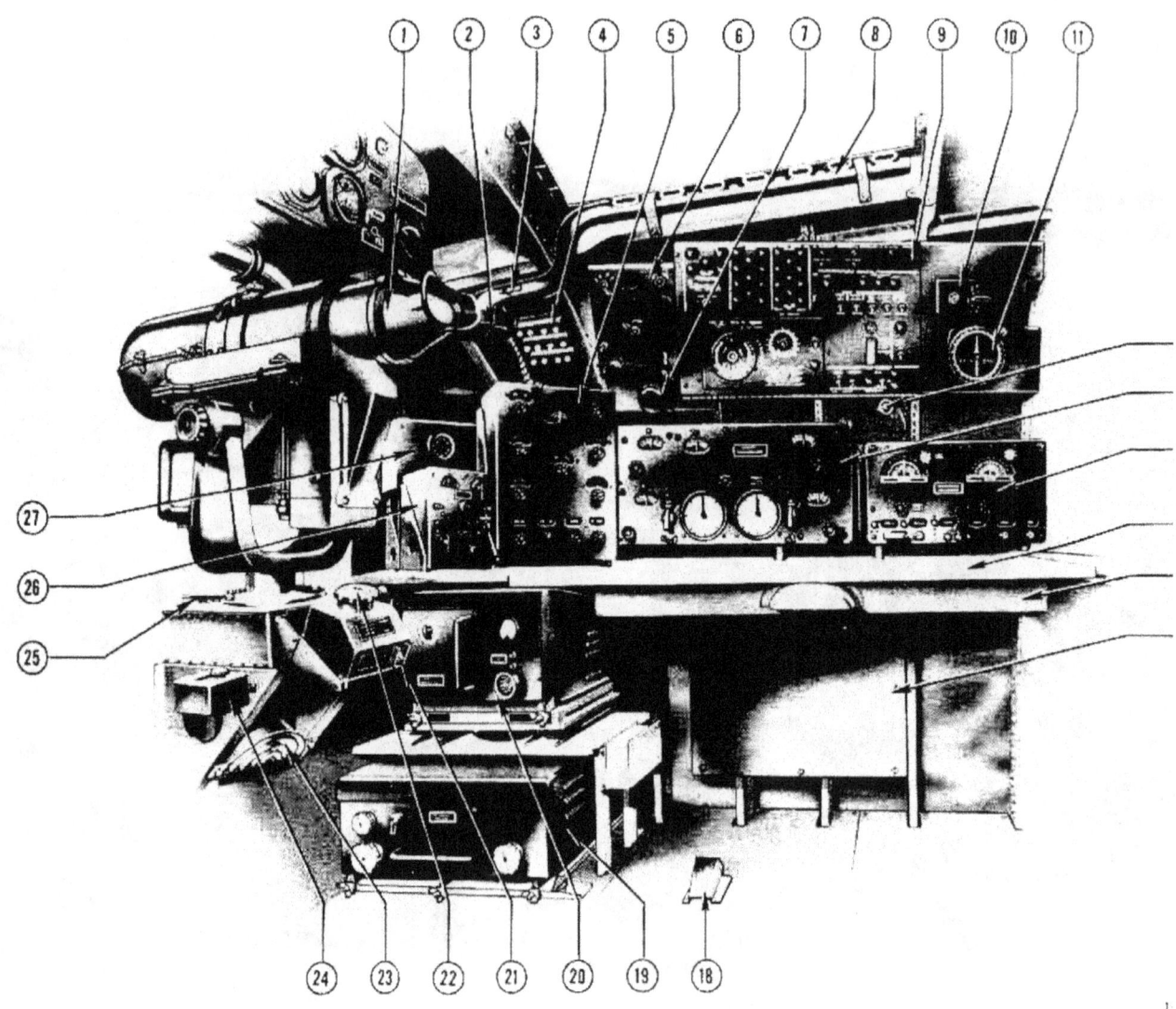

1. ID-218/APS-23 Indicator*
2. Heat and Vent Outlet
3. Astrodome Defrost Shut-off Valve
4. Spare Lamps
5. C-413/APS-23 Control Unit*
6. AN/ARN-6 Radio Compass Control Panel
7. Defrost and Ventilating Air Control
8. Astrodome Defroster Outlets
9. Bomb Control Panel
10. Interphone Panel
11. Radio Compass Indicator
12. Bomb Release Button
13. CP-21/APA-44 Ballistics Computer*
14. CP-22/APA-44 Mileage Computer*
15. Chart Table
16. Chart Table Drawer
17. J-166/APA-44 Junction Box*
18. Microphone Switch
19. AM-166/APA-44 Amplifier Unit*
20. PP-185/APA-44 Power Supply Unit*
21. Auto-pilot Control Transfer Switch†
22. Auto-pilot Turn Control Knob†
23. Heat and Vent Floor Outlet
24. C-416/APS-23 Control Unit*
25. J-218/APS-23 Main Junction Box*
26. C-293/APA-44 Tracking Control*
27. ID-168/APA-44 Airspeed Indicator*

*B-45A-5 Airplanes AF47-37 and AF47-39 thru AF47-96
†B-45A-5 Airplanes AF47-37 thru AF47-96, and B-45C Airplanes

The B-45A/C position for the bombardier-navigator featured controls for the radar, bomb release, auto pilot plus the chart table for navigation.

This is the bomb release panel as mounted in the bombardier-navigators position. Not only could a release sequence be selected but release altitudes and bomb types could also be entered.

engines were running the 115 volt ac alternators, one per engine, came online these being fitted to Nos.1 and 3 engines. The electrical system provided power to the lights, booster pumps, starters, fuel shut off valves, armament and communications equipment, bombing system, camera, automatic pilot, bombing system, nose wheel steering, trim tabs, rudder- elevator boost, ATO ignition units, air conditioning, pressurisation, emergency hydraulic pump, fire detectors and extinguisher, escape deflector flaps plus electrical instrumentation and transmitters.

On later build aircraft electrical supplies also controlled the sequence valves for the landing gear doors plus the inverters for the operation of the automatic pilot, radar equipment and drift meter. The alternators in all versions operated the radar equipment, heaters for wind shield anti-icing, defrosting and surface control boost systems.

The aircraft was well equipped with lighting that covered both interior and external lighting. The latter included the navigation lights that could be used for signalling purposes, when the tip tanks were fitted they had navigation lights fitted as the wing light were obscured. Fuselage identification lights were also fitted above and below, these too could be used for signalling. Formation lights were also installed for the rare occasions when this was practised, other external lights included a landing light mounted in the front of the left engine nacelle while the taxi light was mounted on the left hand undercarriage leg. The internal lighting in the aircraft included lighting for all the panels at the crew stations, lights in the passage way alongside the pilots towards the nose compartment, while in the bomb bay and unpressurised compartments there were lights to assist the ground crew in their maintenance tasks. A further light is installed in the nose wheel bay this being visible through a window at floor level in the pilots compartment, it was used to check the position of the leg.

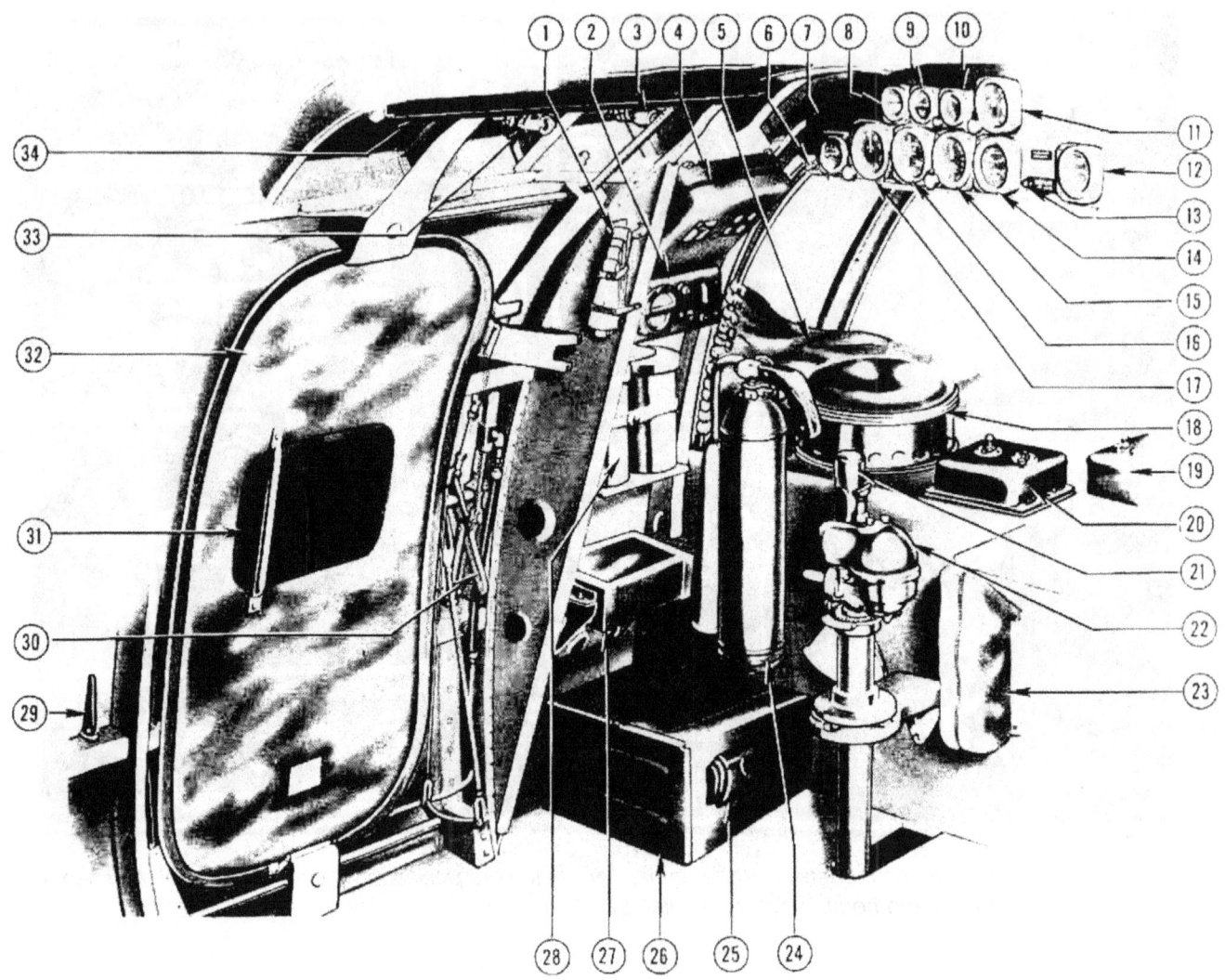

1. Parachute Static Line
2. Radar Pressurization Control Panel
3. Fluorescent Light
4. First-aid Kit
5. Radome Close-out Curtains
6. Driftmeter Power Switch**
7. Free Air Temperature Gage
8. Oxygen Flow Indicator
9. Oxygen Pressure Indicator
10. Clock
11. Cabin Pressure Altimeter
12. ID-166/APA-44 Monitor Voltmeter*
13. Bombardier Auto-pilot Controller Indicator*
14. Radar Steering Meter*
15. Remote-indicating Compass
16. True Airspeed Indicator
17. Altimeter
18. RT-124/APS-23 Receiver-Transmitter
19. Circuit Breaker Box (Radar)
20. Radar Camera Control Box
21. Hand Axe
22. Driftmeter
23. Anti-exposure Suit†
24. Fire Extinguisher
25. Ash Tray
26. Map and Data Case
27. Sextant Stowage Box
28. Disposal Containers
29. Main Entrance Hatch Control
30. Main Entrance Hatch Emergency Release
31. Window§
32. Main Entrance Hatch
33. Compartment Light
34. Astrodome Close-out Curtain

*B-45A-5 Airplanes AF47-37 and AF47-39 thru AF47-96
**B-45A Airplanes
†B-45C Airplanes
§B-45A-5 Airplanes AF47-77 thru AF47-96, and B-45C Airplanes

In the centre of this diagram is the main entrance hatch in the forward fuselage. In an emergency this could be used for escape purposes although a set of deflector plates would be deployed to assist escape when the emergency handles were operated.

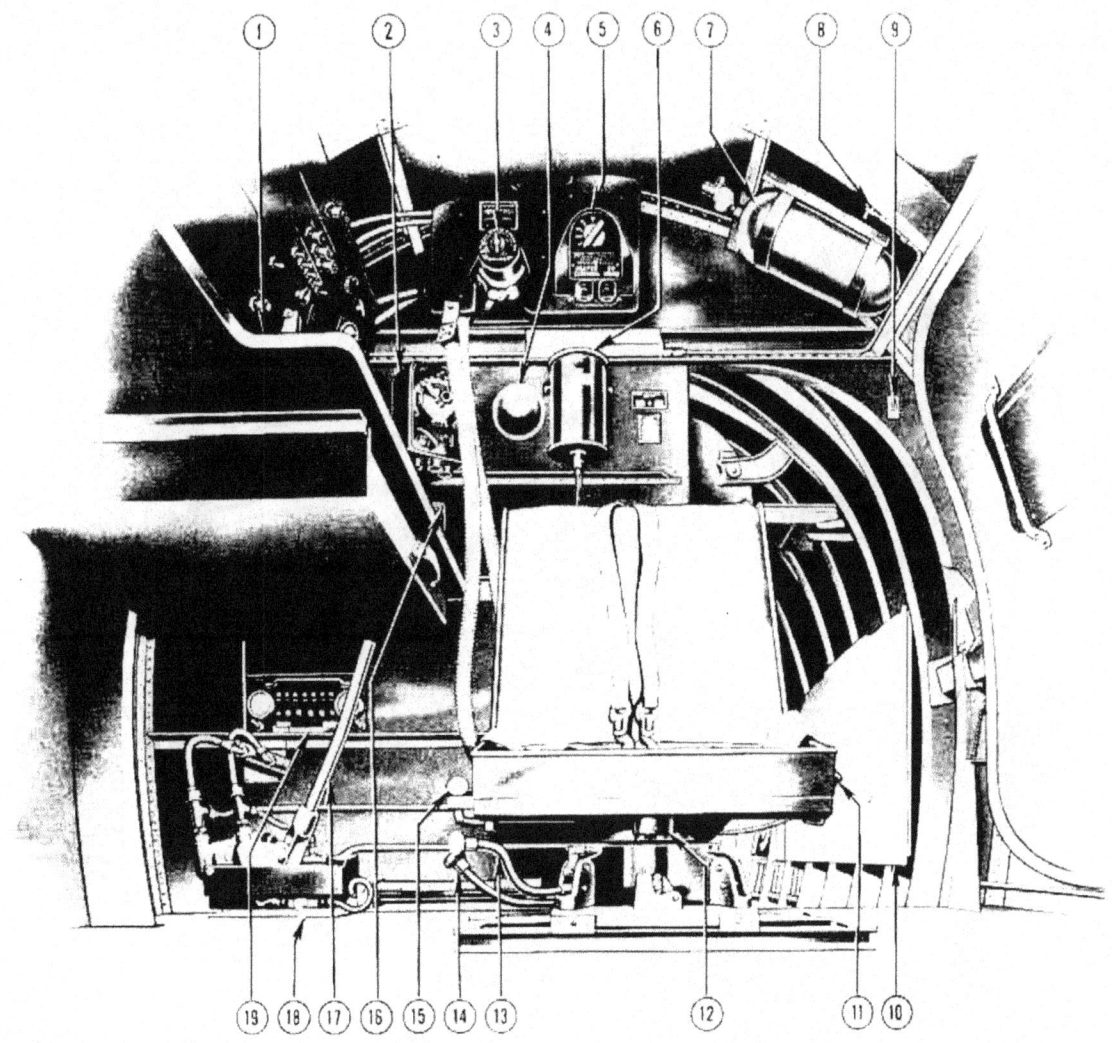

1. Chart Table
2. Camera Intervalometer Control
3. Oxygen Regulator
4. Alarm Bell
5. Heated Clothing Control Panel
6. Nose Gear Emergency Hydraulic Reservoir
7. Portable Oxygen Bottle
8. Refiller Valve—Portable Oxygen Bottle
9. Passageway Light Switch
10. Ditching Panel (Carried on overwater flights only)§
11. Shoulder Harness Lock Control
12. Seat Swivel Control
13. Seat Vertical Control
14. Seat Lateral Control
15. Emergency Escape Control
16. Landing Gear Emergency Operation Instruction Placard
17. Hand-pump—Landing Gear Emergency Release
18. Manual Check Valve—Emergency Landing Gear Lowering System
19. SN-47/APS-23 Synchronizer†

*On B-45A-5 Airplanes AF47-37 and subsequent, located on right side of pilot's walkway
†B-45A-5 Airplanes AF47-37, and AF47-39 thru AF47-96
§B-45A-1 Airplanes, B-45A-5 Airplanes AF47-23 thru AF47-61, and B-45C Airplanes AF48-1 thru AF48-6

This view is looking to the rear of the bombardier-navigators compartment. Not only was this crewman involved with navigation and bomb dropping he also managed the landing gear hand pump and the manual release for undercarriage lowering.

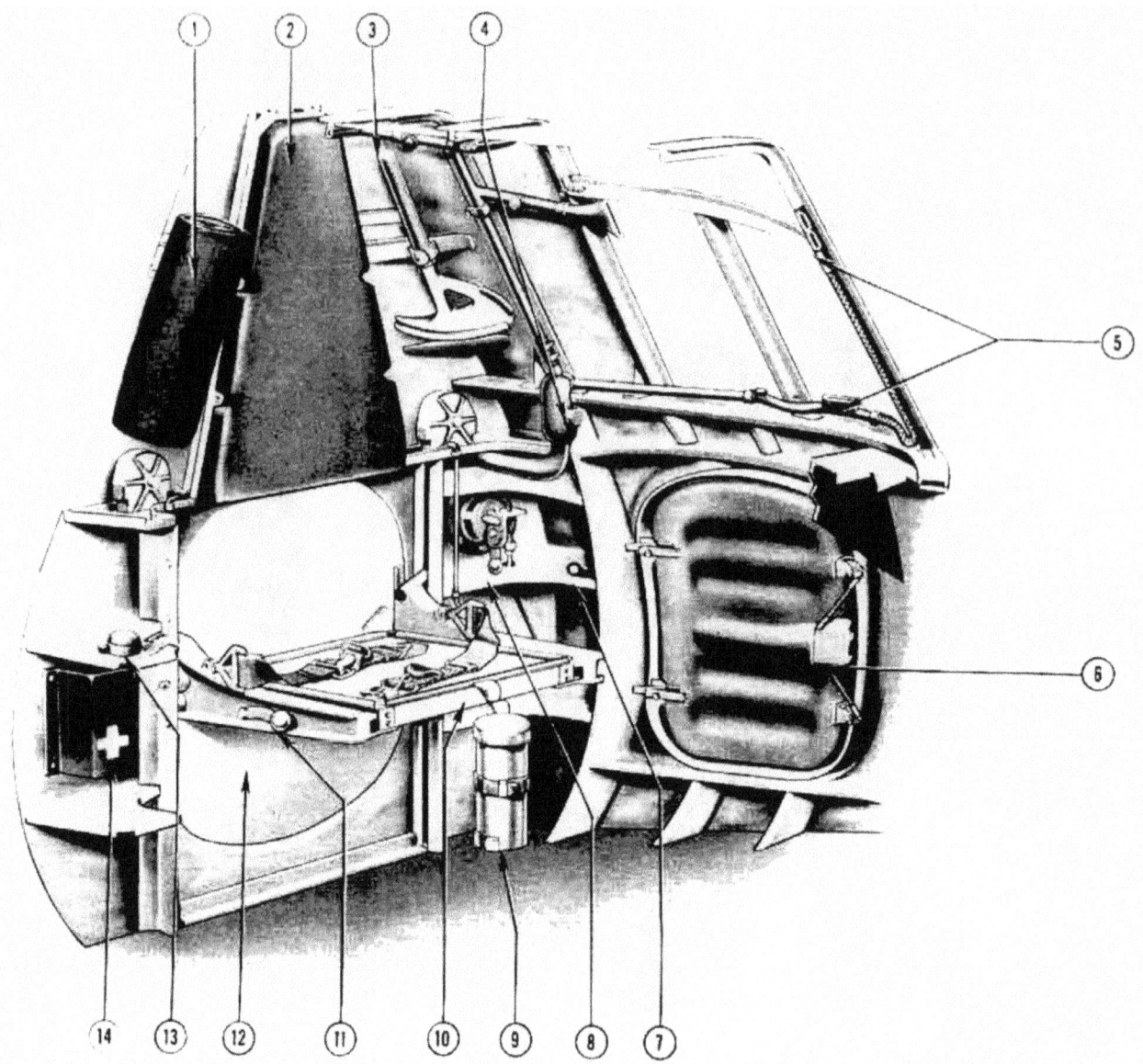

1. Ditching Belt*
2. Head and Back Rest
3. Hand Axe
4. Air Shut-off Valve
5. Defroster Outlets
6. Escape Hatch Release Handle
7. Ditching Belt Attaching Hook
8. Cabin Air Emergency Dump Valve
9. Disposal Container
10. Seat Horizontal Adjusting Handle
11. Seat Vertical Adjusting Handle
12. Cabin Access Door
13. Alarm Bell
14. First-aid Kit

*B-45A-1 Airplanes, B-45A-5 Airplanes AF47-23 thru AF47-61, and B-45C Airplanes AF48-1 thru AF48-6

The tail gunners position was no palace as it included a retractable seat, emergency equipment plus the escape hatch which had a set of external deflector plates fitted to assist in an emergency.

Avionics.

One of the major avionics systems fitted to the B-45 was the auto pilot, the Type E-4, this being managed by a stowable control panel at the pilots position. The auto pilot could be used in conjunction with the automatic approach equipment this being the airborne part of the instrument landing system. On the later build

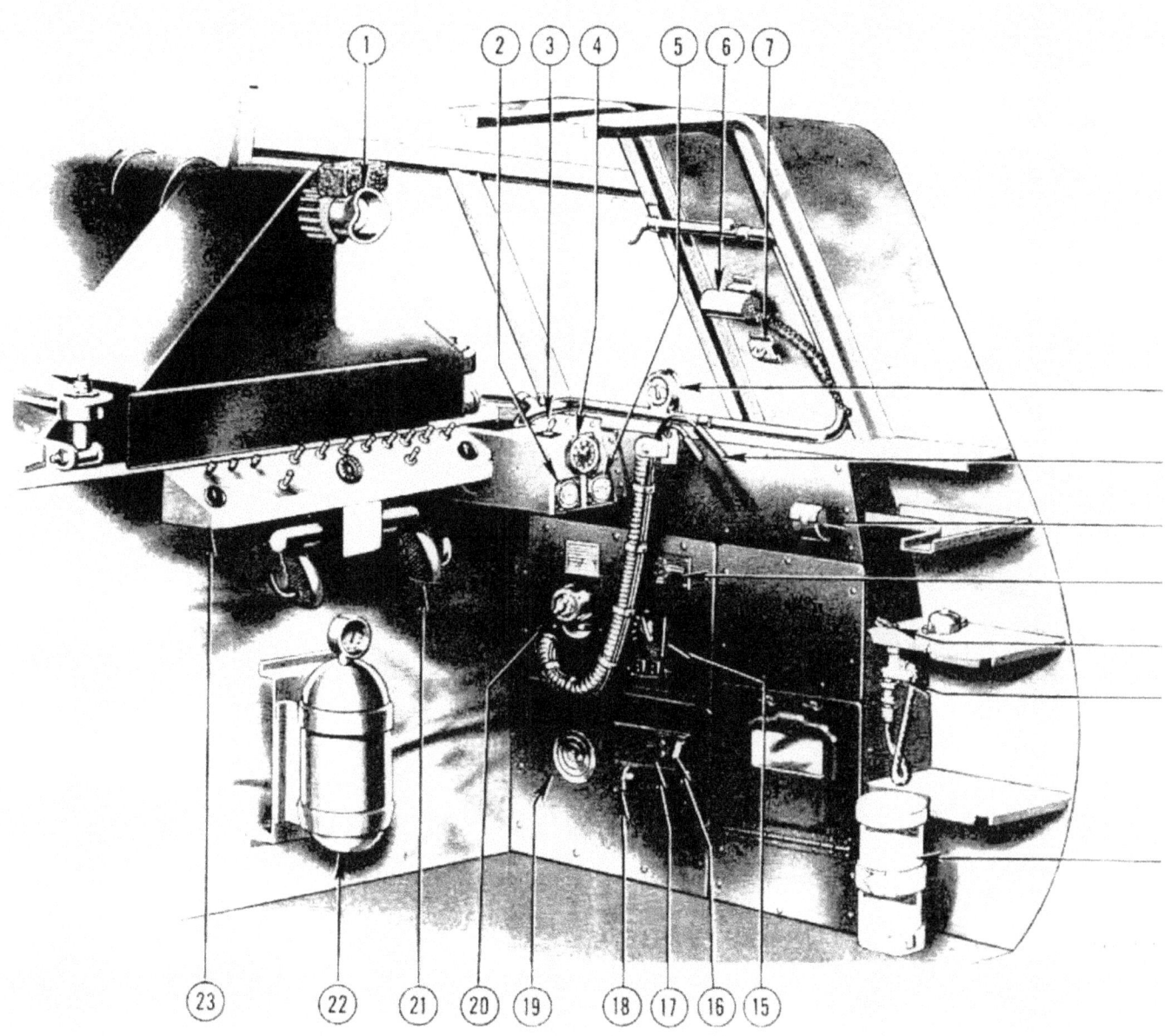

1. Gun Sight
2. Oxygen Flow Indicator
3. Cabin Pressure Switch
4. Cabin Pressure Altimeter
5. Oxygen Pressure Indicator
6. Cabin Light
7. Spare Lamps
8. Heat and Vent Outlet
9. Radio Jacks
10. Ash Tray
11. Interphone Panel
12. Ditching Belt Attaching Hook
13. Refiller Valve—Portable Oxygen Bottle
14. Disposal Container
15. Heated Clothing Panel
16. Emergency Escape Switch
17. Circuit Breakers
18. Cabin Temperature Rheostat
19. Heat and Vent Outlet
20. Oxygen Regulator
21. Turret Controller
22. Portable Oxygen Bottle
23. Turret Control Panel

Looking aft in the gunners position the main turret control panel is visible plus the gunsight. Also in this zone were items of emergency equipment plus a big no-no in todays society- an ash tray.

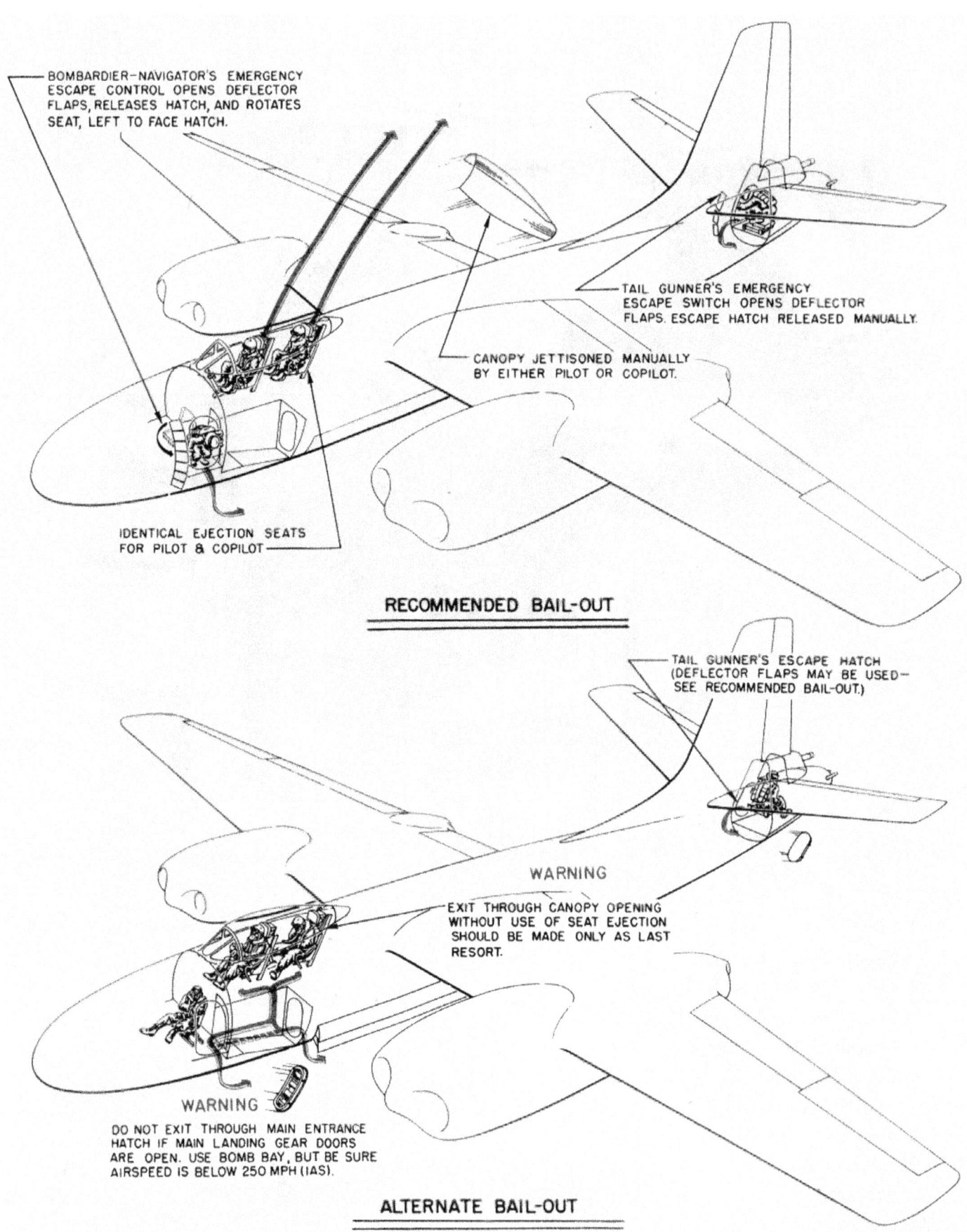

This diagram illustrates the preferred method of escaping from a stricken B-45 although a more hazardous alternative is also shown.

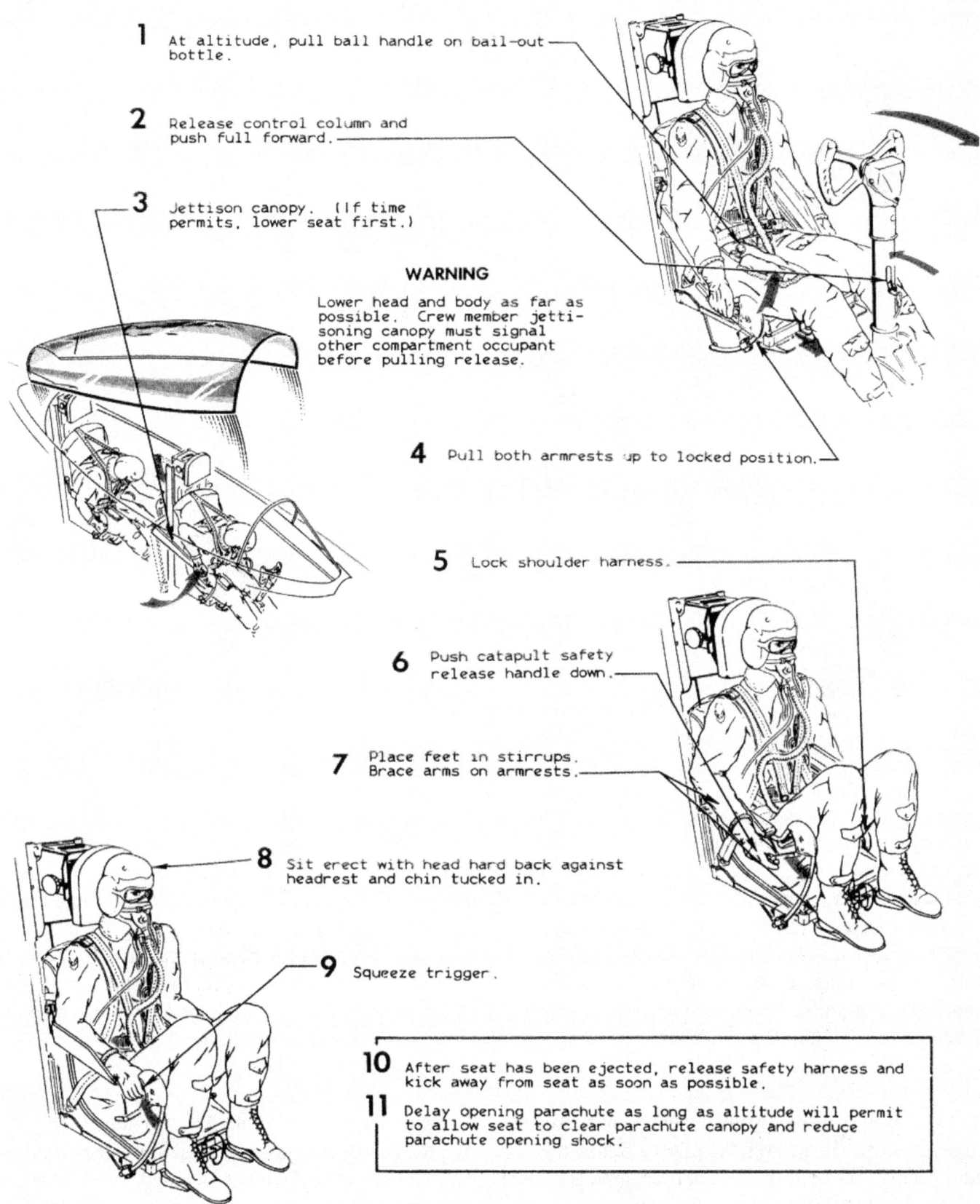

1. At altitude, pull ball handle on bail-out bottle.
2. Release control column and push full forward.
3. Jettison canopy. (If time permits, lower seat first.)

WARNING

Lower head and body as far as possible. Crew member jettisoning canopy must signal other compartment occupant before pulling release.

4. Pull both armrests up to locked position.
5. Lock shoulder harness.
6. Push catapult safety release handle down.
7. Place feet in stirrups. Brace arms on armrests.
8. Sit erect with head hard back against headrest and chin tucked in.
9. Squeeze trigger.
10. After seat has been ejected, release safety harness and kick away from seat as soon as possible.
11. Delay opening parachute as long as altitude will permit to allow seat to clear parachute canopy and reduce parachute opening shock.

Both the pilot and co-pilot were mounted on ejection seats and this diagram illustrates the method of egress although the canopy had to be jettisoned before the seats could leave.

aircraft the auto pilot could also be engaged with the radar navigation system through a steering connector in the bombardier's compartment, when engaged it allowed the bombardier to steer the aircraft on its

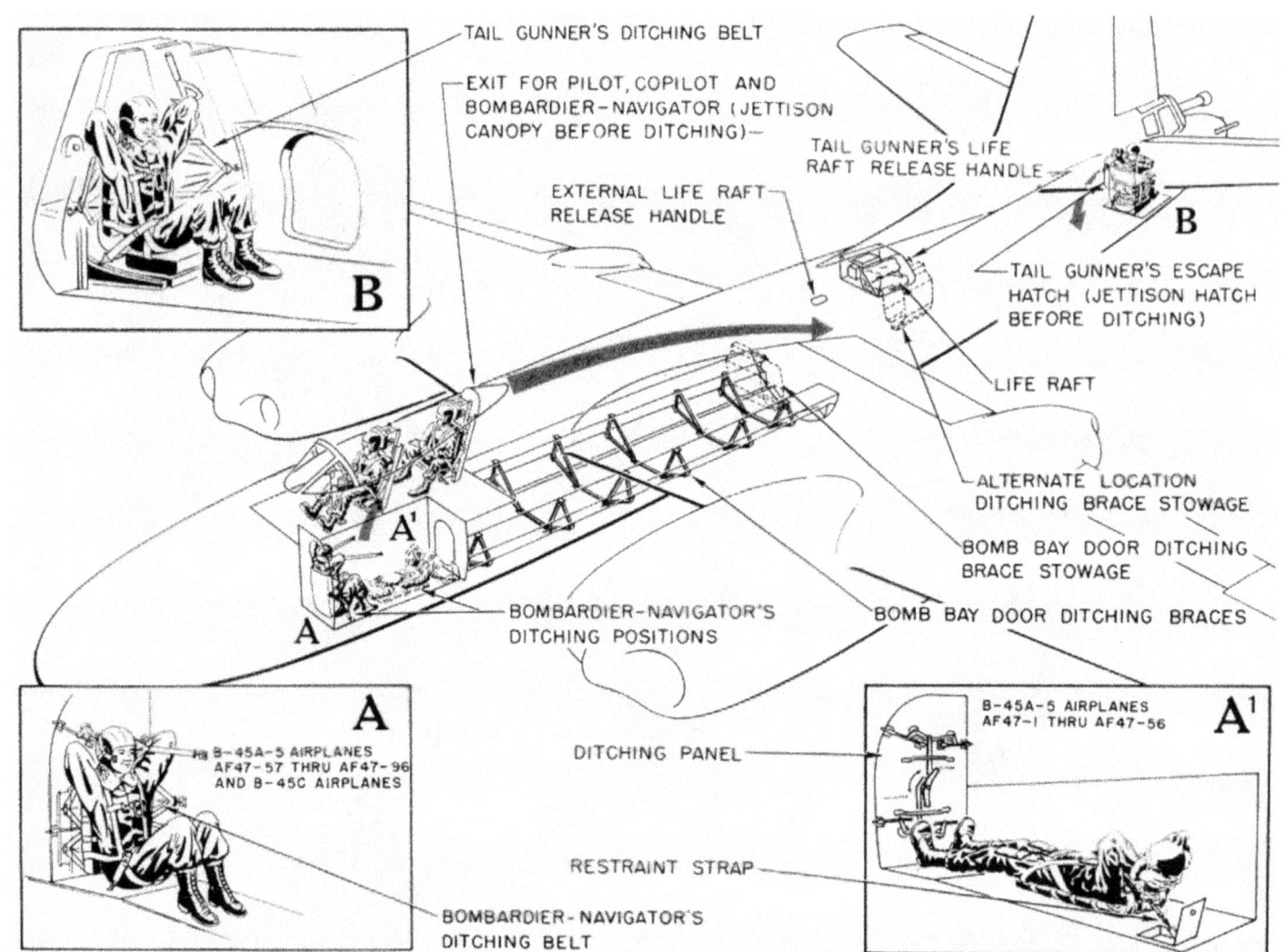

It was intended that the B-45 crew could ditch their stricken bomber however in reality should a B-45 be in such dire straits it is highly unlikely that the crew would not have time to rig such equipment.

bombing run. The main limitation to the auto pilot was that it could only be engaged when in level flight as engagement in a turn would cause the aircraft to divert off course. When the auto pilot was engaged the side stick controller could be used to fly the aircraft. The auto pilot could also be managed under barometric control for height maintenance although this could be used unless the elevator servo was engaged.

The B-45 was also fitted with an automatic approach control system that allowed the pilot to follow the radio beams generated by the localised approach glide path beams. To engage the approach control the autopilot needed to be disengaged while the controller needed to be selected to either localiser or approach. As the aircraft intercepted the localiser beam it turned to follow the beam down towards the runway. Once the aircraft had reached the centre of the beam the controller was moved from localiser to approach. While the B-45 could in theory land using this system the pilot was required to disengage just before touch down and undertake a manual landing. Should there be a problem with either end of the localiser beam the aircraft would immediately begin to climb at an angle of 2.5 degrees. Auto pilot control could also be transferred to the bombardier although this could not occur if the auto pilot was disengaged.

The avionics installed in the B-45 included the AN/APQ-24 bombing and navigation radar while the communications equipment included the AN/ARC-3, for command purposes, the AN/ARC-8 used by the co-pilot for long range communication and the AN/ARN-6 radio compass. Other equipment installed included the RC-103/ AN/ARN-5A for instrument approach, the SCR-695-B IFF, the AN/AIC-2A interphone for aircraft crew communications, the RC-193-

(A) marker beacon receiver plus the AN/CRT-3 emergency dinghy radio.

Other Systems

The B-45 Tornado was also fitted with other equipment that was intended to either improve the performance of the aircraft or improve the safety of the crew. The first system was the Jet Assisted Take Off, JATO, units. These external rocket pods were carried under the nacelles and were capable of generating a maximum of 4,000 lbs of thrust for up to a minute. The switches were fired using the switches mounted on the pilots panel, when ignition was selected both bottles should ignite and burn until all of the fuel was consumed although there was an off option available which would cancel the rocket burn. Once the JATO units were expended the pilot could operate the jettison switch to drop the bottles.

All crew member were provided with a method of escape should such be necessary. The pilots were sat upon ejection seats , both being housed under a jettisonable canopy. The canopy could be jettisoned from either pilots position , there was also an external release handle located just aft of the canopy centreline on the right hand side of the fuselage. Once the canopy had been jettisoned the pilots could use their ejection seats to escape, although these were of the catapult type , under all normal circumstances they were effective.

The other members of the crew, the navigator and the tail gunner had to undertake manual bail outs from their respective compartments, both being fitted with hydraulically powered wind deflectors that assisted the crewmen in their escape. When the bombardier-navigator starts the escape process the wind deflectors are deployed while the crewman's seat was swivelled towards the entrance door whose pins were released allowing the door to spring clear. Should the tail gunner need to escape operation of his emergency control deployed the wind deflectors although the escape hatch, located on the left hand side of the fuselage, needed to be operated manually. In order that the navigator should feel supported by his fellow crew members there was a reinforced panel that could be placed across the walkway between the pilots cockpit and the nose section the purpose of which was to stop the fuselage flooding if the glazed section of nose section fractured.

While ditching of a stricken B-45 was not the usual option provision for such an event was made however the entire process was convoluted affair. Both the bombardier and tail gunner were supplied with restraint straps that were attached to the aircraft's structure. However before using these restraints the crew were enjoined to install the bomb bay ditching kit. This comprised of six supports that needed to be installed at colour coded matching points on the bomb bay doors. Further equipment in the form of a life raft was also available. The raft , complete with an emergency radio, was housed in the unpressurised compartment just aft of the bomb bay on the left hand side. When the raft was released it automatically inflated and remained attached to the aircraft by a mooring line that would be released once the crew were aboard.

Bombing and Navigation Systems plus defensive armament

The B-45 Tornado was capable of carrying twenty seven 100 lbs bombs although the aircraft was capable of carrying a single 22,000 lbs bomb. Operation of the bomb doors was hydraulic using electrical selection and control. Should it be needed a camera could be installed on the rear bulkhead of the bay this being monitored by the bombardier- navigator if required. Release of the bomb load could be managed from the control panel in the nose compartment and allowed the operator to release the weapons in sequence, singly or in salvoes.

The aircraft also had defensive armament in the tail position this comprising of a pair of M-24 0.50 inch machine guns each being provided with 600 rounds per gun. The guns were controlled remotely by the gunner housed in a pressurised compartment forward of the turret. The guns were automatically charged using an independent pneumatic charging system. The guns were guided using an MD1 hemispherical optical sighting system which included a gun camera. For longer range firing the radar guidance system could be used , the gunner being able to switch to the optical system if required.

This nose view is representative of the prototypes and the early production B-45's thus the pilots canopy is a clear blown item while the navigators position has only three frames supporting the glazing.

The B-45 nose leg retracts aft into its bay although the rear door shuts after opening and closing.

The main undercarriage was mounted next to the engine nacelle, note the mounting of the small fairing.

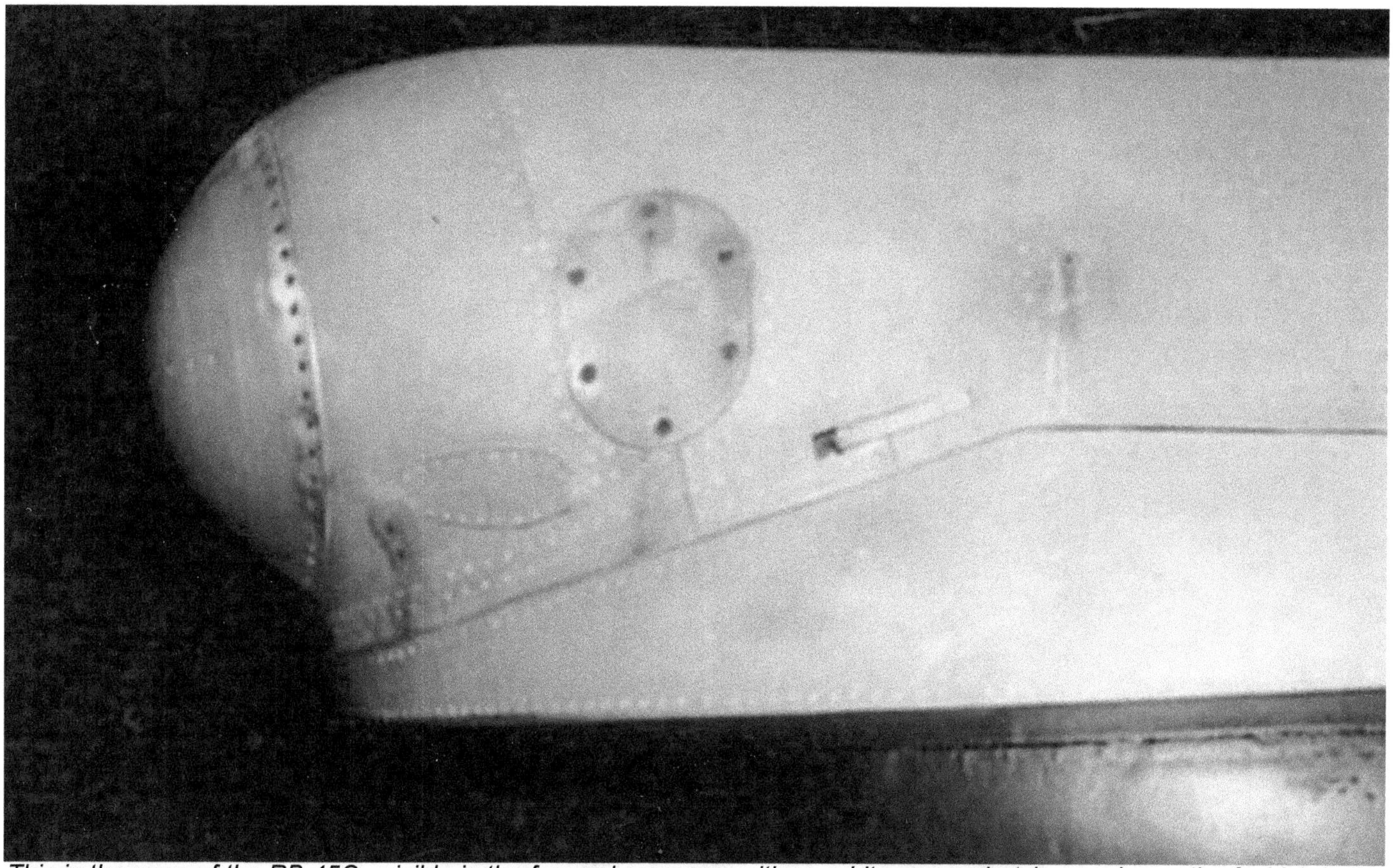

This is the nose of the RB-45C , visible is the forward camera position and its access hatches underneath of which is the radar radome.

While engineers refuel this B-45 of the 47th BW it should be noted that this aircraft is fitted with water methanol tanks under the engine nacelles. These were used to boost performance when the aircraft was heavily loaded or operating under hot and high conditions by injecting the mix into the engines.

The main pilots panel in the B-45 was quite a cluttered affair as this view shows as the engine gauges are dominant although the main basic flight controls are centred behind the control wheel.

This is the outboard flap section as fitted to all versions of the B-45 Tornado. Also visible are the main undercarriage doors as the main door has been lowered for access.

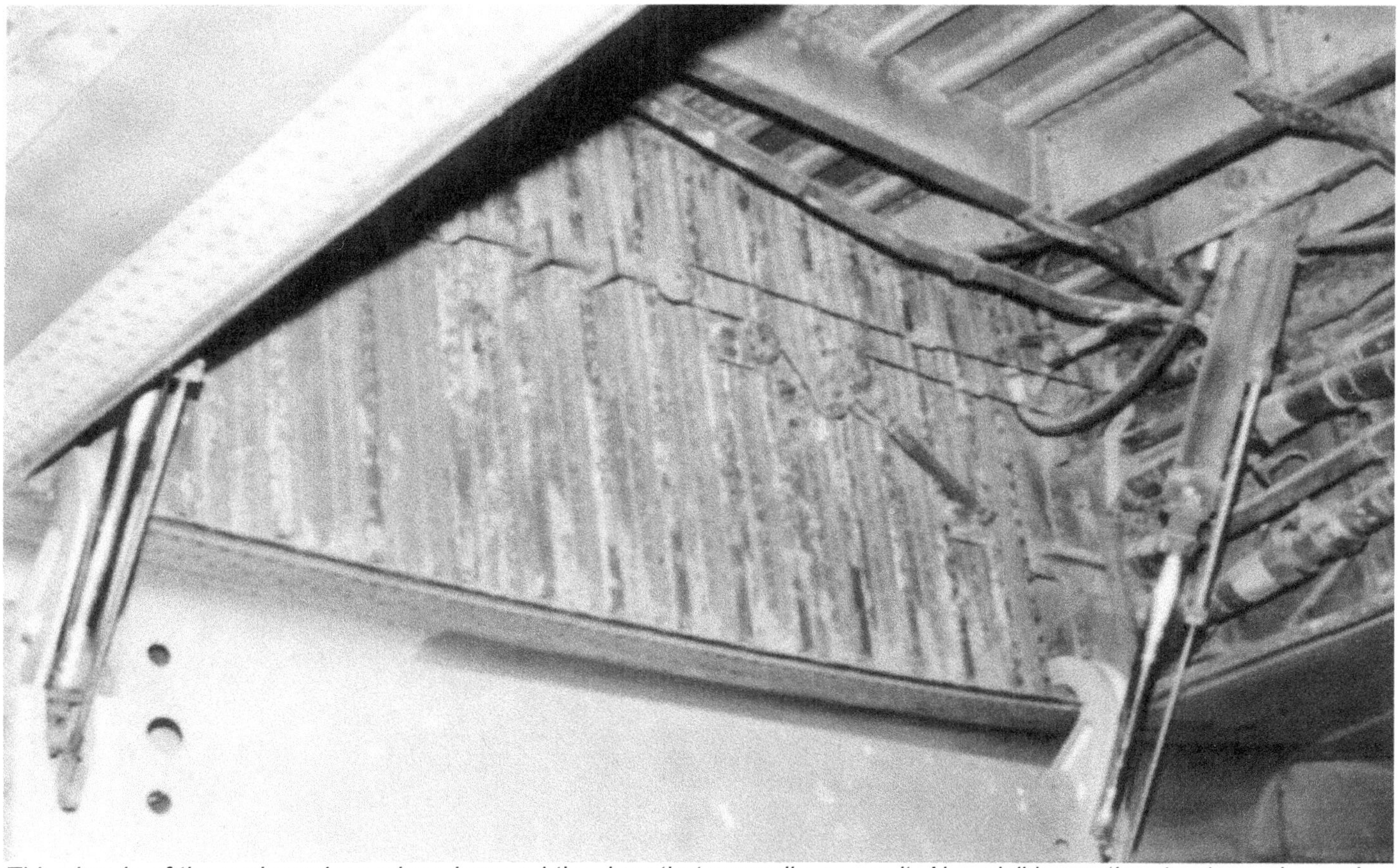

This view is of the main undercarriage bay and the door that normally covers it. Also visible are the structure, pipework and retract jacks for the door.

This is another view of the main undercarriage bay looking aft. Clearly visible are the hydraulic pipes to the retraction jacks plus part of the fuel system piping.

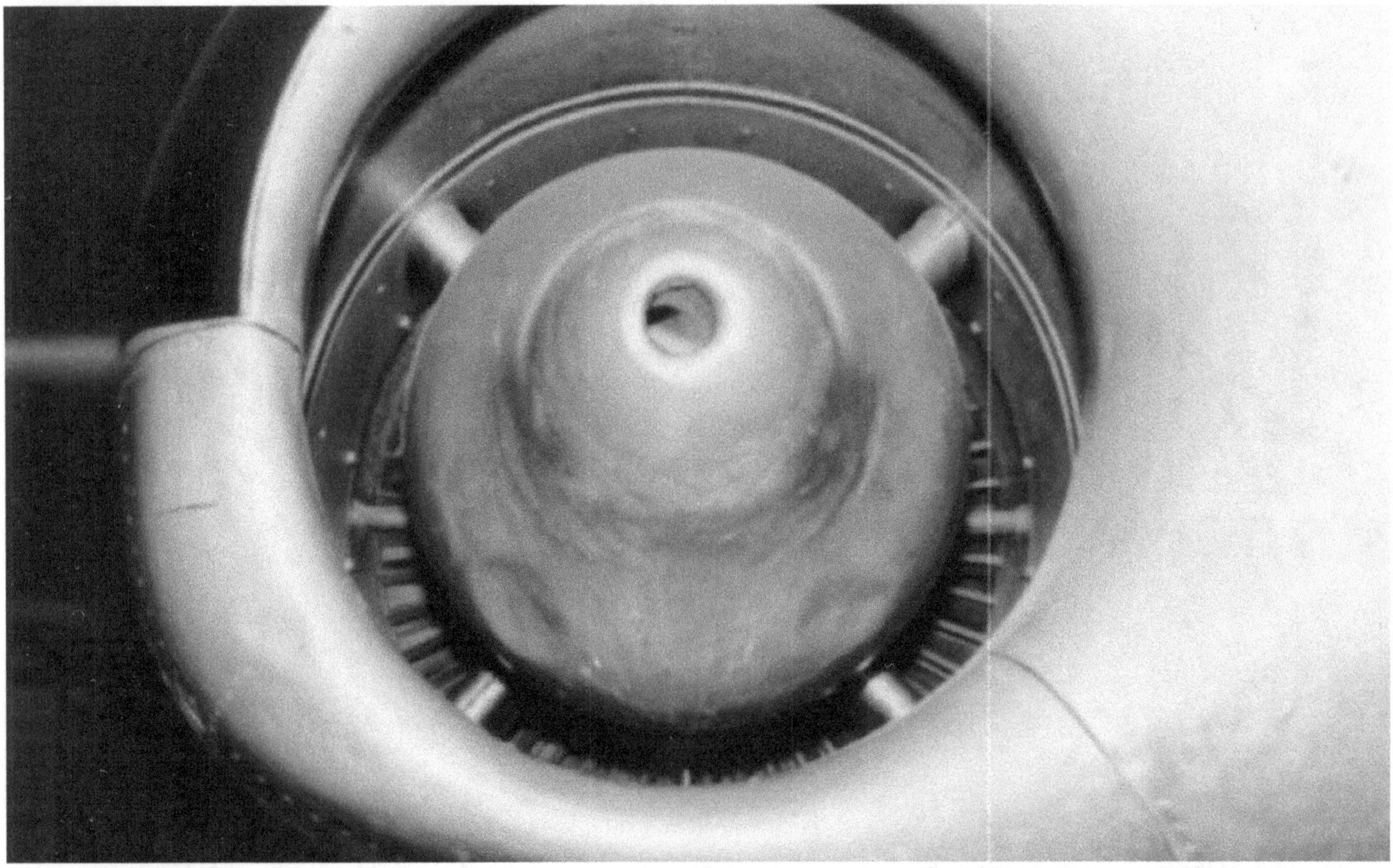

This is the outboard engine as fitted to the J47 powered versions of the B-45. When fitted with the J47 engine the aircraft became a more sprightly performer although when fully loaded it could struggle until some fuel was burnt off.

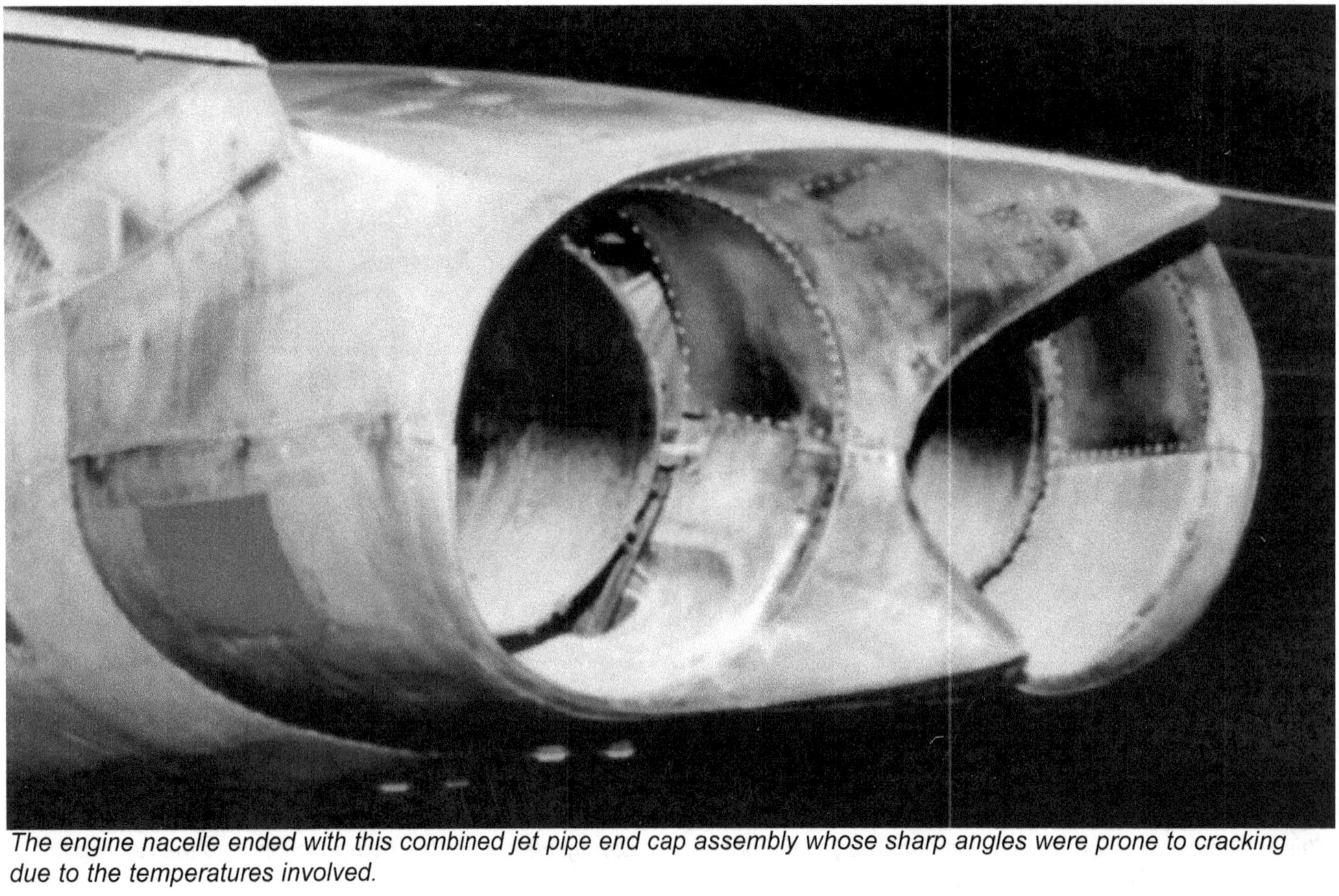

The engine nacelle ended with this combined jet pipe end cap assembly whose sharp angles were prone to cracking due to the temperatures involved.

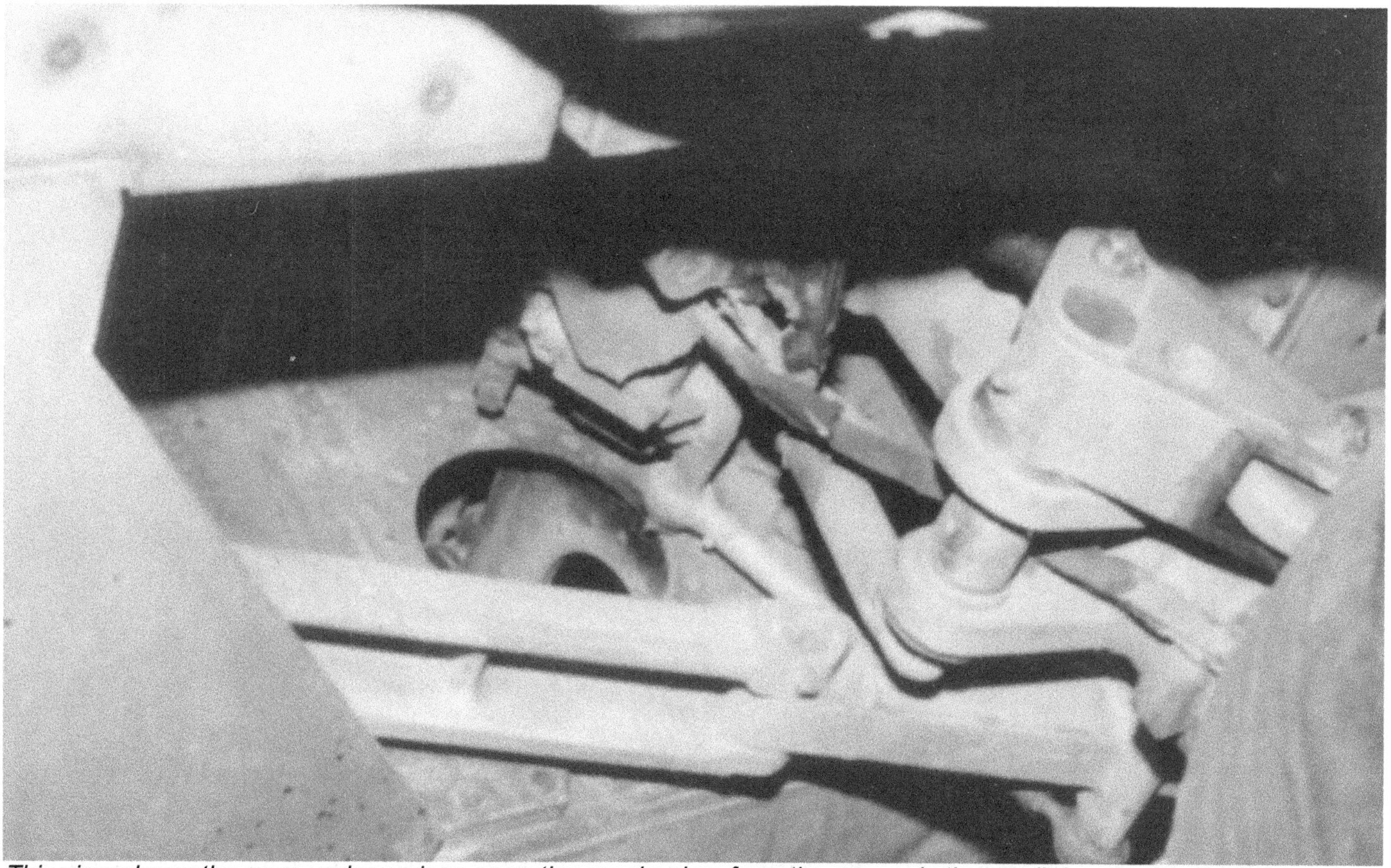

This view shows the nose undercarriage operating mechanism from the rear, only the small door beside the leg remained open when the undercarriage was extended.

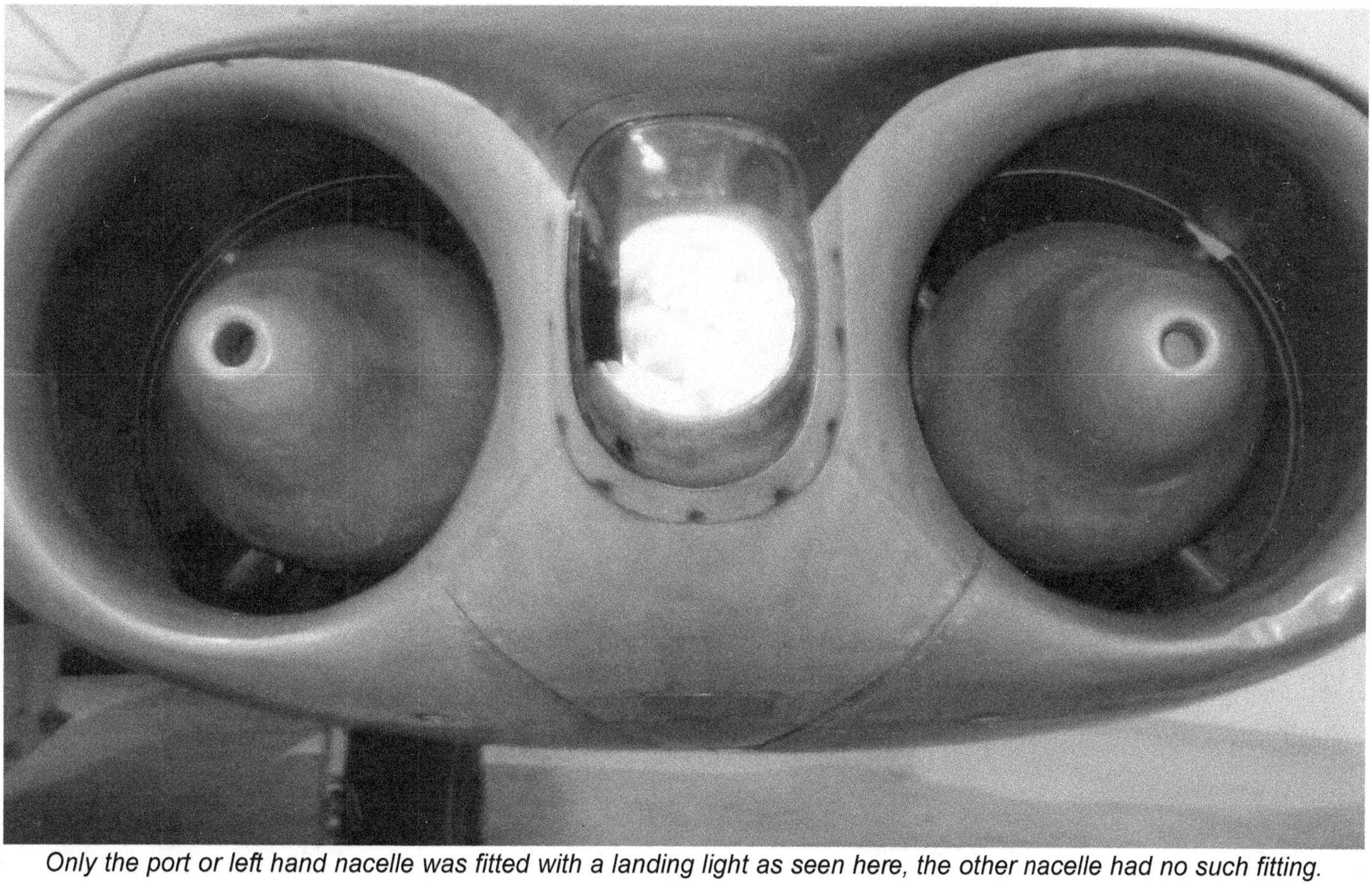

Only the port or left hand nacelle was fitted with a landing light as seen here, the other nacelle had no such fitting.

This is the top of the main undercarriage leg, this shows the swivel point quite clearly.

This a B-45 undergoing maintenance for which purpose the engine access doors have been lowered. Note the load spreader between the doors.

Flight line engineering staff give their charge a final polish before flight. Except for the black painted aircraft used in Korea the B-45 series remained unpainted.

This view of an RB-45C nose shows quite clearly the nose camera position and the viewing head for the periscope above the nose.

NAA B-45/RB-45 TORNADO- CHAPTER FOUR
THE RB-45C TORNADO DESCRIBED

The RB-45C was structurally similar to the earlier bomber version although it was described as a high speed, high altitude photo reconnaissance aircraft. Changes from the bomber version included photo reconnaissance equipment housed in the aft fuselage and nose section. The RB-45C was intended for night reconnaissance, high and low level photography plus mapping and charting. For night reconnaissance duties photo flash bombs could be carried in the forward bomb bay. The crew in this version consisted of a pilot, co-pilot, tail gunner and photo navigator who also covered the duties of bombardier and radar operator. The RB-45C was also fitted with in-flight refuelling equipment which extended the operating range of the aircraft. The fuselage was divided into seven compartments of which the three crew compartments were pressurised while the forward camera compartment, the bomb bays and the aft camera compartments are unpressurised. The bomb bays could be accessed in flight although the doors need to be shut and the bays empty with the remainder of the fuselage depressurised. It was not possible to enter the aft camera bay during flight. Other changes from the earlier bomber included an updated AN/APQ-24 bombing and navigation radar, AN/APN-9A while provision was made for the installation of the AN/APN-3 system.

The engines installed in the RB-45C were from the J47 series and were mounted thus: a dash 7 or 13 in one engine position in each nacelle while the other slot was filled with either a dash 9 or 15. Each engine had an independent pressurised scavenge oil filter system that contained 9.2 US gallons of usable oil. Throttle controls were mounted in a pedestal on the right hand side while a similar set was fitted at the co-pilots position both sets of levers being interconnected. The water injection system became operative when the relevant throttle lever was positioned between 95 and 100% at which point a detent micro switch opens to allow operation. While the fuel system fitted to the RB-45C was an improved version of

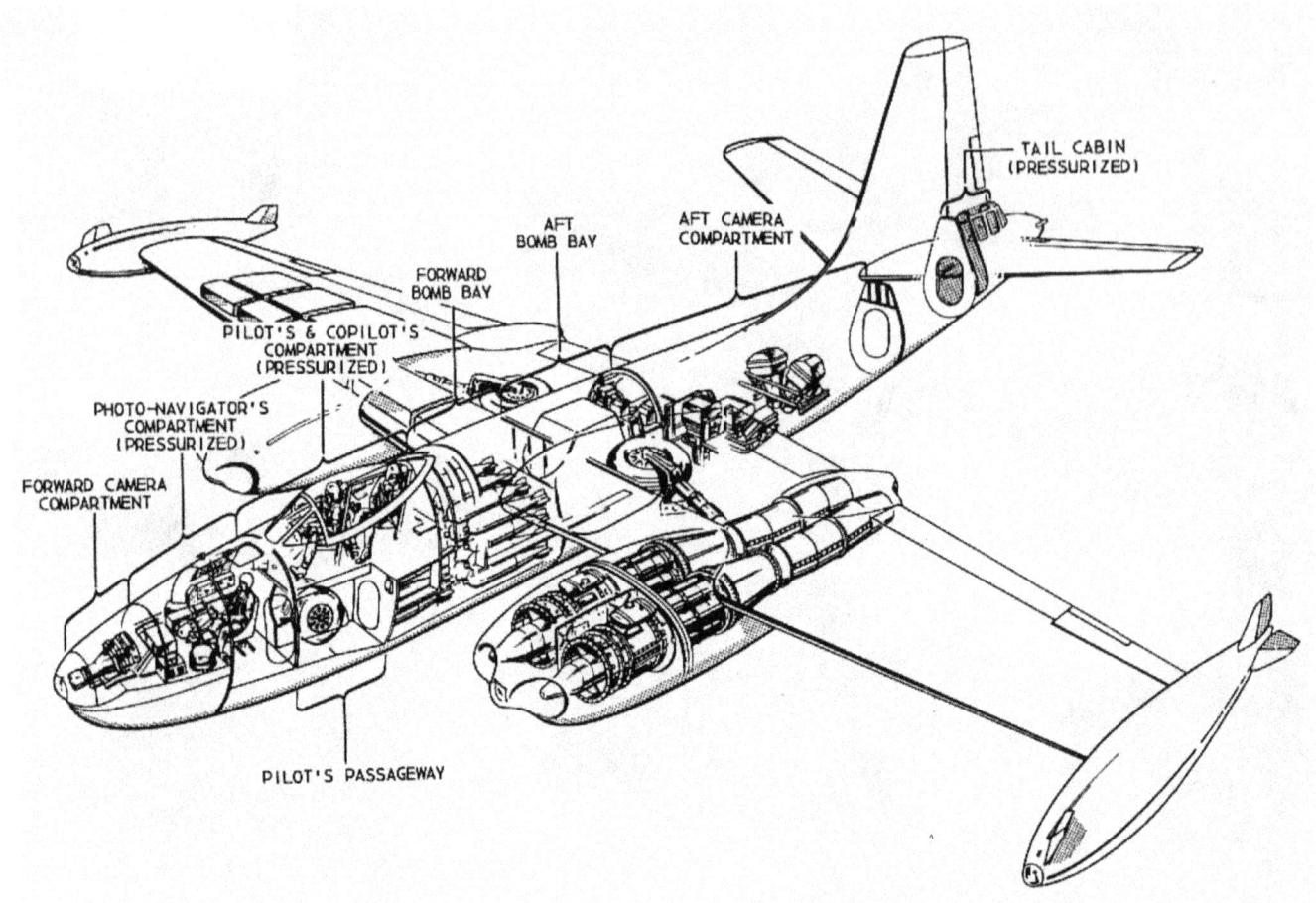

This diagram illustrates the various compartments within the RB-45C Tornado and deliniates those that are pressurised.

that installed in the bomber variant however the emergency fuel system regulator was disconnected. Engine starting was via a single switch per engine that was labelled start and stop while the off position was in the centre mid position. The starter unit for each engine was a combined starter generator that acted in the former role up to an engine speed of 23%. As the engine speed increases the starter circuit was disengaged with the generator coming on line at 50% speed.

Should it be needed the RB-45C engines had a water methanol injection system available to increase the available thrust for heavy weight take offs. The water for this system was carried in 214 US gallon tanks suspended from the ATO mountings underneath the engine nacelles. Each tank supplied an alcohol-water mix directly into the relevant engines combustion chambers ,feed being courtesy of an air driven pump there being one per engine. When the injection system was operated a trimmer tab in each jet engine nozzle operated to reduce the size of the nozzle. This

reduction in nozzle size allowed for maximum exhaust temperature to be maintained. All four injection systems are controlled by a single switch although should one system fail the remainder would continue to operate. To maintain an equal amount of thrust from the nacelle with the failed engine the entire water injection feed was diverted to the remaining powerplant which was capable of maintaining the increased thrust for a short period. Once the water tanks were emptied they could be jettisoned by the pilots using the ATO release switch.

The RB-45C fuel system was based on that installed in the bomber however it did include an extra tank in the fuselage plus a droppable tank carried in the rear bomb bay this holding 1,200 US gallons of fuel. Further fuel could be carried in the forward bomb bay whose tank could carry a further 1,200 US gallons while wingtip tanks , each holding 1,125 US gallons, were fitted as standard. When the bomb bay fuel tanks were fitted their contents were fed directly to a cross feed pipe that fed directly into the engine fuel

1. Fluorescent Light
2. Auto-pilot Engaged - Power-off Indicator
3. Auto-pilot Trim Indicator
3A. A-C Gyro Instrument Warning Light
4. Radar Steering Meter
5. Radio Compass
6. Flap Position Indicator
7. Landing Gear Door Indicator Light
8. Landing Gear Position Indicators
9. Landing Gear Position Indicator Light
10. Forward Engine Compartment Fire Warning Indicators
11. Fire Extinguisher Switch
12. Aft Engine Compartment Overheat Indicators
13. Fire Detector System Test Switches
14. Clock
15. Accelerometer
16. ATO Indicators
17. Oxygen Pressure Gage
18. Oxygen Flow Indicator
19. Water Injection System Indicators
20. Water Injection System Switch
21. Stand-by Compass
22. Remote-indicating Compass
23. Attitude Gyro
24. Bomb Door Indicators
25. Rate-of-Climb Indicator
26. Tachometers
27. Exhaust Temperature Indicators
28. Hydraulic Pressure Gage
29. Hydraulic Fluid Level Indicator
30. Fuel Pressure Gages
31. Aileron Trim Indicator
32. Rudder Trim Indicator
33. Elevator Trim Indicator
34. Instruments Inoperative
35. Cabin Pressure Altimeter
36. Control Column Release Lever
37. Free Air Temperature Gage
38. Turn-and-Bank Indicator
39. Altimeter
40. Fuel Flowmeter and Totalizer Indicator
41. Elevator Trim Auxiliary Switch
42. Refueling Boom Disconnect Switch
43. Camera Initiation Switch
44. Auto-pilot Release Button
45. Radio Microphone and Interphone Button
46. Nose Wheel Steering Trigger Switch
47. Fuel Gages - Right Wing Tanks
48. Fuel Gages - Left Wing Tanks
49. Fuel Gages - Large Bomb Bay Tanks
50. Wing Tip Tanks "Empty" Indicators
51. Fuel Filter De-icer Switch
52. Fuel Filter Ice Warning Indicator
53. Fuel Gage - Fuselage Tank
54. Oil Temperature Indicators
55. Air-to-Air Refueling Indicators
56. Camera Pre-exposure Warning Light
57. Photo Operation Indicator Light
58. Oil Pressure Gages
59. Pilot's Check List
60. Glide Path and Runway Localizer Indicator
61. Marker Beacon Indicator
62. Airspeed Indicator

The pilots compartment in the RB-45C was very similar to those in the earlier bomber versions. The main banks of gauges measure engine performance and handling while the primary flight instruments are mounted in a block in the centre of the panel.

1. Fuel System Control Panel
2. Horn Cutoff Switch - Cabin Pressure (Some Airplanes)
3. Bomb Door Switch
4. Surface Control Boost Switch
5. Taxi Light Switch
6. Landing Light Switch
7. Code Selector
8. Fuselage Lights Switch
9. Navigation Lights Switch
10. Engine Air Intake Anti-icing Switch
11. Windshield Anti-icing Switch
11A. Tail Cabin Pressure Switch
12. Canopy Anti-icing Switch
13. Pilot's Air and Windshield Defroster Control
14. Main Cabin Pressure Switch
15. Pitot Heater Switch
16. Wing Anti-icing Switch
17. Tail Anti-icing Switch
18. Emergency and Parking Brake Levers
19. Formation Lights Switch
20. Emergency Brake Boost Switch
21. Fuselage Lights Indicator
22. Auto Code Switch
23. Tail Anti-icing Rheostat
24. Surface Control Boost Test Lights
25. Fuel Panel Lights Rheostat
26. Wing Anti-icing Rheostat
27. Wing Flap Control
28. Power Controls
29. Spare Lamps - Fuel System Control Panel
30. Power Control Friction Lock
31. Emergency Alarm Switch
32. ATO Release Switch
33. ATO Ignite Switch
34. Engine Starter Switches
35. Data Case
36. Battery Switch
37. Horn Cutoff Switch - Landing Gear
38. Aileron Boost Cutout Switch

This pedestal houses many of the system controls managed by the pilot.

1. Heat and Vent Outlet
2. Command Radio Control Panel
3. Bomb and Fuel Tank Salvo Control Switch
4. Salvo Circuit Indicator Light
5. Pneumatic System Bleeder Valve
6. Bomb and Fuel Tank Salvo Selector Switch
7. Radio Compass Control Panel
8. Interphone and Mixer Switch Panel
9. Instrument Approach Control Panel
10. Cockpit Light
11. Controls Lock
12. Emergency Brake Hydraulic System Pressure Gage
13. Oxygen Regulator
14. Heated Clothing Control Panel
15. Emergency Hydraulic Selector Valves
16. Circuit Breaker Panels
17. Canopy Manual Emergency Release
18. Radio Frequency Channel Card
19. Cabin Air Valve
20. Compass Light Rheostat*
21. Wing Tip Tank Mechanical Release
22. Hydraulic Main System Pressure Control Valve
23. Cabin Temperature Rheostat
24. Landing Gear Selector Control
25. Landing Gear Lock Emergency Release
26. Trim Tab Control Stick
27. Cabin Temperature Manual Override Switch
28. Auto-pilot Engaging Handles

*AF48-35 and subsequent

The pilots left hand panel was also a cluttered affair and included the bomb and fuel tank release controls.

1. Auto-pilot Release Button
2. Radio and Interphone Microphone Button
3. Elevator Trim Auxiliary Switch
4. Rudder Bars
5. Copilot's Check List
6. Auto-pilot Engaged - Power-off Indicator
7. Oxygen Flow Indicator
8. Airspeed Indicator
9. Turn-and-Bank Indicator
10. Attitude Gyro
11. Remote-indicating Compass
12. Rate-of-Climb Indicator
13. Fluorescent Light
13A. A-C Gyro Instrument Warning Light
14. Altimeter
15. Oxygen Pressure Indicator
16. Heat and Vent Floor Outlet

The co-pilots main panel was a lot less cluttered as the engine gauges were all on the main pilots panel.

1. Heated Clothing Control Panel
2. Cockpit Light
3. Oxygen Regulator
4. Generator Switches
5. Ammeters
6. Heat and Vent Outlet
7. Automatic Pilot Controller
8. A-C Voltmeter Selector
9. A-C Voltmeter
10. Alternator Selector Switch
11. Alternator Warning Lights
12. Alternator Master Switches
13. Canopy Manual Emergency Release
14. Canopy Defroster Outlets
15. Alternator Selector Control Switch
16. D-C Voltmeter
17. Disposal Container
18. Main Hydraulic System Filler Hose
19. Portable Oxygen Bottle
20. Landing Gear and Door Emergency Manual Controls
21. Pneumatic System Pressure Gage
22. Pneumatic System Filler Valve
23. Main Hydraulic Reservoir Filling Hand-pump
24. Bomb Door Manual Control
24A. Surface Control Boost Test Shutoff Switch
25. Surface Control Boost Test Switches
26. D-C Voltmeter Selector
26A. A-C Gyro Instrument Switch
27. Generator Overvoltage Lights
28. A-C Frequency Meter
29. Inverter Switch
30. Inverter Warning Lights
31. Circuit Breaker and Fuse Panel
32. AN/APX-6 IFF Transpondor
33. AN/APX-6 IFF Control Panel*
34. Interphone Amplifier Auxiliary Gain Control
35. Cockpit Light:
    Fluorescent Light - AF48-11 Through AF48-34
    Red-White Floodlight - AF48-35 and Subsequent
35A. SA-3/A Inertia Switch
35B. IFF Destructor Test Indicator Lights
36. Alarm Bell

*AF48-34 and subsequent

The co-pilots right hand panel included the communications equipment.

60

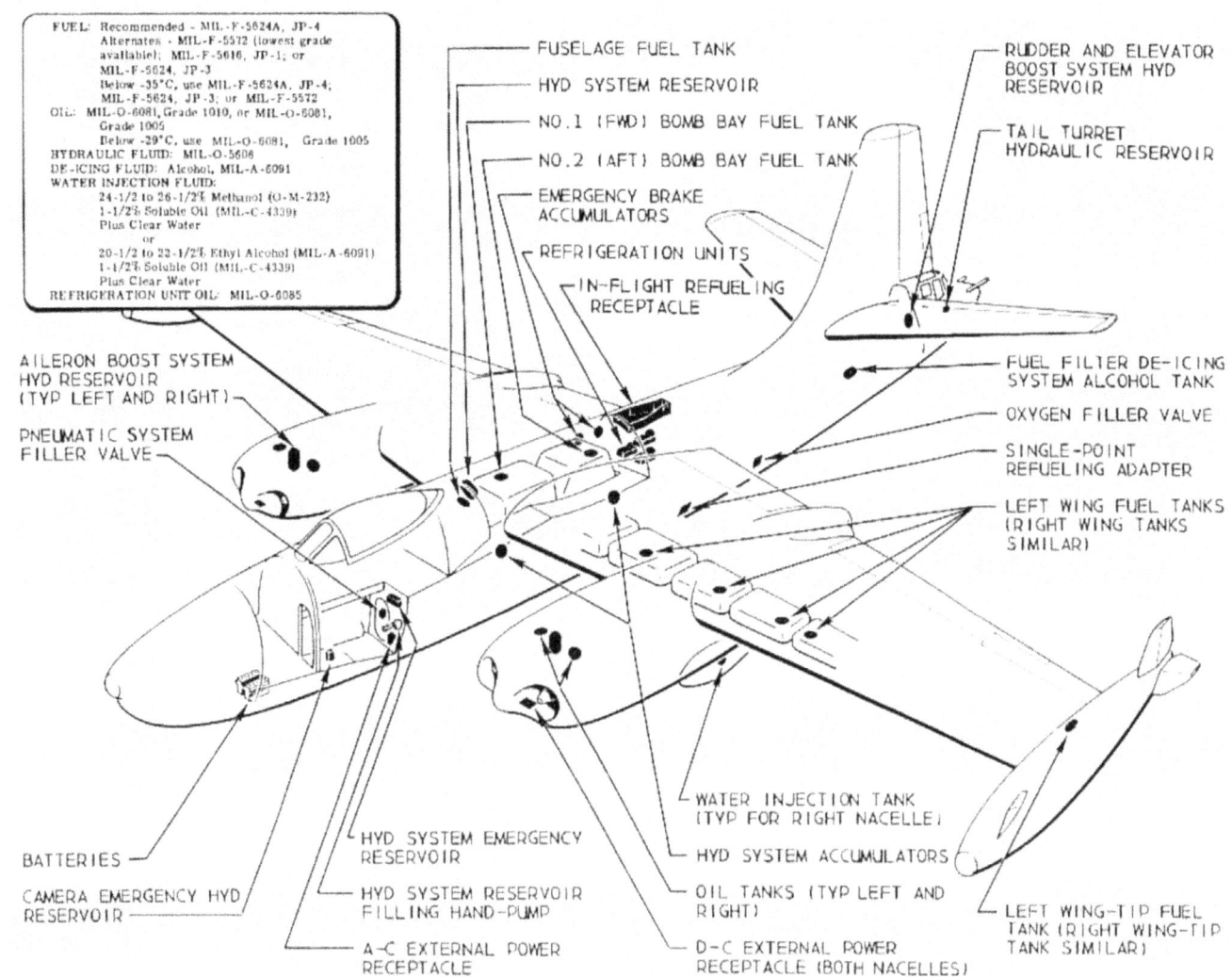

This cutaway shows the location of many of the hydraulic, electrical and conditioning system components. Also clearly shown is the location of the flight refuelling receptacle.

feed system in each nacelle. Should there be a failure of the aircraft electrical system all of the tanks could feed fuel into the delivery system by either gravity or suction methods. The fuel in the wingtip tanks and the bomb bay could also be utilised although only through using suction feed. In a similar manner to the B-45 the RB-45C could also jettison its bomb bay fuel tanks although in contrast to the bomber there was a protective shield that protected the tank when the forward doors were opened. To ensure that the bomb bay tanks were not accidentally dropped on the ground two pins were fitted for safety reasons to each tank, these needed removing before flight to restore the airborne salvo capability. The wingtip tanks could also be released using either the mechanical or salvo release, both controls being mounted in the pilots cockpit.

While the RB-45C has the same single point pressure refuelling system as fitted to the bomber version that in the reconnaissance aircraft was protected by the use of primary and secondary fuel control valves that would automatically switch each tank to the next in the sequence otherwise major structural damage could occur.

The reconnaissance version of the aircraft was also fitted with an in-flight refuelling system that utilised the AN/APN-68 radar to guide it onto the tanker aircraft. The RB-45C was one of the earliest aircraft to be fitted for boom refuelling. The receptacle and slipway was located on the top of the fuselage just forward of the fin. When connected to the tanker the dispensed fuel travelled up the receiver line into the single point refuel system from where it will refill all of the aircraft's fixed tankage plus the wingtip and bomb bay tanks if selected while refuel speed was 300 US gallons per minute. Once the hydraulically operated

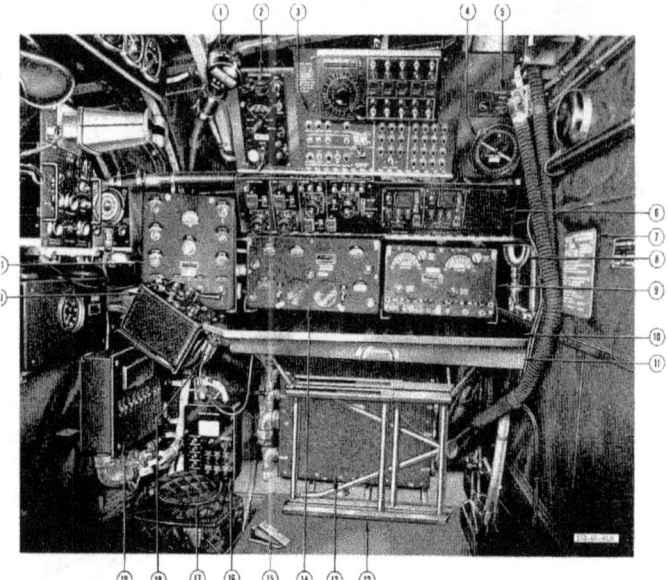

1. Canopy Defroster Outlets
2. Power Controls
3. Heat and Vent Outlet
4. Cockpit Light
5. Interphone Panel
6. Radio Circuit Breakers
7. Canopy Seal Pressure Gage
8. Canopy Seal Pressure Regulator
9. Radio Compass Receiver
10. AN/ARN-5A Localizer Receiver
10A. Refueling Selector Valve Switches
11. In-flight (Air-to-Air) Refueling Control Panel
12. Emergency Brake Boost Switch
13. Fuel Amplifier
14. Emergency Brake Levers
15. Cabin Air Blower Control Switch
16. Fluorescent Light

1. Heat and Vent Outlet and Astrodome Shutoff Valve
2. AN/ARN-6 Radio Compass Control Panel
3. Secondary Camera Control Panel
4. Radio Compass Indicator
5. Interphone Panel
6. Primary Camera Control Panel
7. Landing Gear Emergency Operation Instruction Placard
8. Chart Table Light
9. CP-22/APA-44 Mileage Computer
10. Chart Table
11. Chart Table Drawer
12. Main Entrance Ladder
13. J-166/APA-44 Junction Box
14. CP-21/APA-44 Ballistics Computer
15. Microphone Switch
16. Radar Junction Box
17. CN-66/APS-23 Gyroscope
18. Manual Bomb Release Switch
19. J-218/APS-23 Junction Box
20. C-293/APA-44 Tracking Control
21. C-413/APS-23 Control Unit

The pilots left hand panel was centred around the in flight refuel panel and the auto land system.

slipway was opened fire protection in the form of a CO_2 discharge became operative while post refuelling the receiver line was purged using gaseous nitrogen. The primary flight refuel panel was located in the co-pilots cockpit although the pilot had the refuel disconnect switch mounted on the control wheel plus a set of indicator lights so that the refuel could be monitored. To assist the tanker boom operator in seeing the refuel slipway at night the RB-45C was fitted with lights each side of the slipway and two lights mounted aft of the cockpit canopy which shone aft.

The electrical, hydraulic and flight controls were similar to those fitted to the B-45 bombers although the RB-45C was fitted with improved flight surface boost systems. One each was installed in the port and starboard aileron systems while the third was fitted into the rudder and elevator system. The rudder/elevator boost system was powered by a pair of electrically driven pumps while the aileron boost units drew their power directly from the aircraft hydraulic pumps.

Unlike the bomber the reconnaissance Tornado had its navigators compartment outfitted with extensive equipment in support of this role as this veiw shows.

Photo Reconnaissance Equipment

The reconnaissance cameras were housed in the fore and aft camera compartment, the forward had one mounting position available while there were three in the aft. To maintain an even temperature in each compartment it was fitted with a conditioning system that also ensured that the camera windows remain ice and frost free at all altitudes. To protect the camera windows they were covered by hatches that were moved using hydraulic jacks. When operating, a vacuum suction system ensures that the film is completely flat during exposure. Should the RB-45C have to undertake night photographic missions the forward bomb bay could be utilised to carry photo flash bombs, to assist the photo navigator in acquiring targets and compute drift offsets. Controls to operate the cameras and associated equipment's were housed in the photo navigators compartment while camera initiation switches were mounted in both the photo navigators compartment and the pilot's positions.

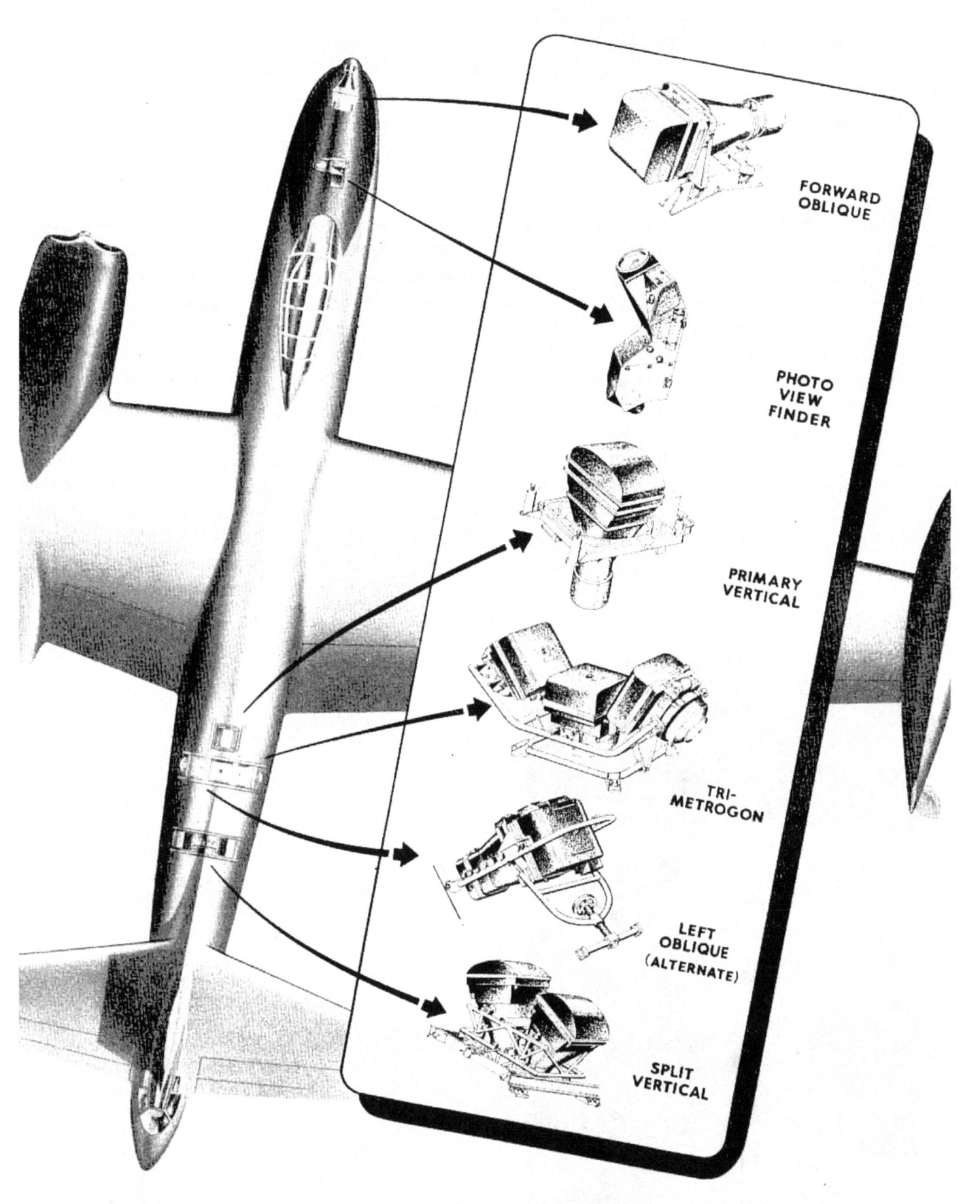

This diagram illustrates the camera positions fitted to the RB-45C. The various camera combinations are outlined in the text.

The camera's installed in the RB-45C included the forward oblique position in the nose compartment, this could either be a K-22A for day reconnaissance this being fitted with either a 12 or 24 inch lens. An alternate installation was the A-6M for filming purposes there being three lenses available, namely 25, 50 or 250 mm. The aft compartment housed the main block of camera's. The single primary vertical mounting could house the T-11, K-22A, K-17C, K-38, K-37 or the S-7A. To ensure that the camera in the primary vertical mounting remained in the vertical plane during flight manoeuvring an A-28 compensating mount could be installed. This unit could compensate for movements up to eight degrees forward, left and right while the aft movement limit was four degrees. Except for the S-7A that was used for filming purposes the remaining camera's could be fitted as needed depending on the mission. Aft of the primary vertical mounting was the Tri-metrogon which mounted three K-17C whose primary task was for charting. If needed there was a position available to mount a left oblique camera, either a K-22A for day reconnaissance or an S-7A movie camera for low level high speed filming. The final mounting was known as the split vertical which could either mount a pair of K-38 camera's each with 24 inch lenses for high altitude day reconniassance or a pair of K-37 each carrying 12 inch lenses for night reconnaissance. Management of the reconnaissance suite was carried out in the photo-navigators compartment using three separate panels. The first covered the supply of electrical power to the camera's, the second was the primary control panel this being backed up by the third which managed the secondary camera controls. The primary control panel allowed the operator to select the speed and modes in which the camera's operated using intervalometers for automatic running or manually using the mode selector switch. Close to the primary panel was the secondary that controlled the camera door switches, bomb door switch, nose camera arming switch, indicators for the various camera positions plus bomb station indicator lights. The electrical panel energised the camera's and the switches for the vacuum pumps that were used to create a partial vacuum in the film magazines that held the film close against the platen. The camera doors covered the compartment windows and

1. Altimeter
2. True Airspeed Indicator
3. Auto-pilot Controller Indicator
4. Clock
5. Free Air Temperature Gage
6. Cabin Pressure Altimeter
7. Oxygen Flow Indicator
8. Oxygen Pressure Indicator
9. ID-166/APA-44 Monitor Voltmeter
10. Visor for R-249/APN-9A (Loran) Receiver-Indicator
11. SCR-718C Radio Altimeter
12. R-249/APN-9A (Loran) Receiver-Indicator
13. ID-168/APA-44 Airspeed Indicator
14. Photo-viewfinder Wide-angle Rheostat
15. Photo-viewfinder Grid Indicator Light
16. Photo-viewfinder Grid Change-over Lever
17. Photo-viewfinder Grid Rheostat
18. Photo-viewfinder Drift Control Crank
19. Photo-viewfinder Power Switch
20. Photo-viewfinder Ground Speed Computer Dial
21. Heat and Vent Floor Outlet
22. Shutoff Valve for Photo-viewfinder Window or Floor Outlet
23. Azimuth Controller for A-28 Stabilized Mount
24. P-3B Camera Control Box
25. Turn Control Knob - Automatic Pilot
26. Controller Selector Switch - Automatic Pilot
27. Photo-viewfinder
28. C-416/APS-23 Control Unit
29. Camera Initiation Switch
30. Photo Operation Indicator Light
31. RT-124/APS-23 Receiver-Transmitter
32. ID-218/APS-23 Indicator
33. Radar Steering Meter
34. Inclinometer
35. Remote-indicating Compass

The photo-navigator in the RB-45C was a very busy person as this illustration shows. His duties included navigation, target selection plus camera management and operation.

TOP *This panel was located in the pilots cockpit and controlled the in-flight refuel system.*
RIGHT UPPER *This panel was also located in the pilots cockpit and controlled the bomb doors, the release of photo flash bombs and their frequency selection.*
RIGHT LOWER *These panels in the photo navigators position controlled camera selection.*

remain closed until the camera's were required. Selection of the relevant switch on the secondary panel opened the required cover panel, it being closed once filming was finished. Should there be a failure of the camera door hydraulic system there was a hand pump available that could be used to open the camera window covers although they could not be closed using this system.

To assist the photo-navigator in his task the RB-45C was fitted with a photo viewfinder this allowed the operator unrestricted vision of the ground forward and below the aircraft. There were two optical systems within the viewfinder these being wide angle and drift system. This unit allowed the operator to check for target location and navigation although both systems were viewed through the same lens. The wide angle system covered a range of 85 degrees in the longitudinal plane while in the vertical it covered 5 degrees aft and 80 degrees forward of the vertical. The drift system covered the area directly below the aircraft and a further fifteen degrees fore and aft from the vertical. To assist the operator the resultant pictures were viewed through a grid overlaid on the viewer which assists in navigation and target selection. For night reconnaissance tasks the forward bomb bay could contain a maximum of 25 T-86 photoflash bombs. A photo trip unit mounted over the centre window of the Tri-metrogon was used in conjunction with the bombs. When the bombs were released the bombs would burst in the air at set altitudes emitting a burst of intense light in the process. This light illuminated the ground below that in turn activated the photo cell in the photo trip unit which fired the K-37 camera. The photo trip unit could also be used in conjunction with the split vertical camera installation although in this case both camera's would be fired. The bombs were armed on the ground with main con-

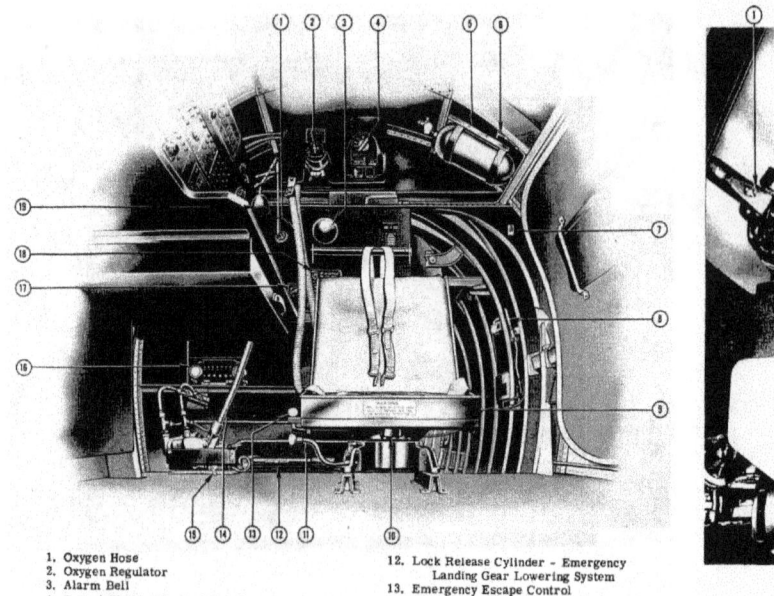

1. Oxygen Hose
2. Oxygen Regulator
3. Alarm Bell
4. Heated Clothing Control Panel
5. Portable Oxygen Bottle
6. Refiller Valve - Portable Oxygen Bottle
7. Passageway Light Switch
8. Camera Emergency Hydraulic Controls
9. Shoulder Harness Lock Control
10. Seat Swivel Control
11. Seat Vertical Control
12. Lock Release Cylinder - Emergency Landing Gear Lowering System
13. Emergency Escape Control
14. Hand-pump - Emergency Landing Gear Lowering System
15. Manual Check Valve - Emergency Landing Gear Lowering System
16. SN-47/APS-23 Synchronizer
17. Chart Table Light Rheostat
18. Landing Gear Emergency Operation Instructions Placard
19. Chart Table Light

The rear of the photo navigators position in the RB-45C was very similar to that of the bomber. Thus it retained the undercarriage emergency controls.

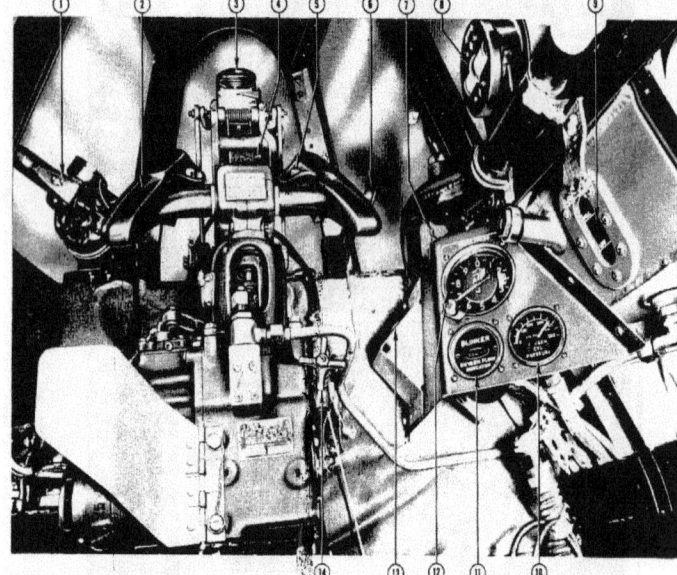

1. Fire Extinguisher
2. Gun Handgrip
3. N-8A Sight
4. Sight Switch
5. Microphone (Interphone) Button
6. Gun Safety Switch
7. Tail Cabin Pressure Switch
8. Heat and Vent Outlet
9. Gun Hydraulic Reservoir
10. Oxygen Pressure Gage
11. Oxygen Flow Indicator
12. Cabin Altimeter
13. Gun Charger Air Pressure Gage
14. Azimuth By-pass Valve

When originally built the RB-45C had a gunner as part of the crew, this the view looking aft. The gunner was later deleted although guns were fitted to those aircraft operating over Korea.

1. Main Entrance Hatch Control
2. Main Entrance Hatch
3. Main Entrance Hatch Emergency Release
4. Fire Extinguisher
5. Parachute Static Line
6. Radar Pressurization Control Panel
7. First-aid Kit
8. AN/APN-68 Radar Control Panel
9. Camera Electrical Control Panel
10. Disposal Containers
11. Camera Circuit Breaker Panel
12. Hand Axe

The equipment around the forward entrance door included emergency equipment plus control panels for various equipments.

1. Oxygen Regulator
2. Compressor Switch
3. Gun Heater Switch
4. Enclosure Defrost Switch
5. Interphone Panel
6. Heated Clothing Control Panel
7. Extension Light
8. Alarm Bell
9. Gun Charger Switch
10. Circuit-breaker Panel
11. Gun Master Switch
12. Cabin Temperature Control Rheostat
13. Extension Light

This panel in the gunners compartment covered gun heating and oxygen controls.

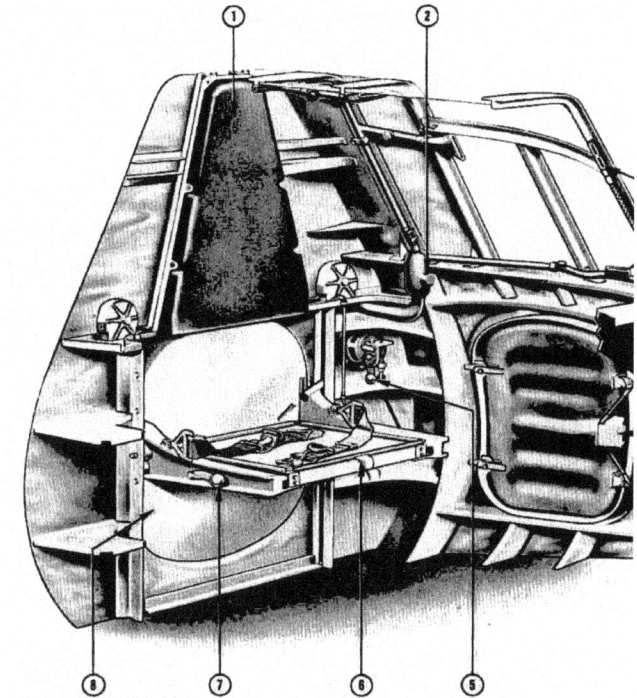

1. Headrest and Back Rest
2. Air Shutoff Valve
3. Defrost Outlets
4. Escape Hatch Release Handle
5. Cabin Air Emergency Dump Valve
6. Seat Horizontal Adjusting Handle
7. Seat Vertical Adjusting Handle
8. Cabin Access Door

The gunnners compartment in the RB-45C was very similar to that of the B-45 and included the uncomfortable seat.

trol being in the photo-navigators compartment switches were available to control the bomb doors, final bomb arming and release. The pilot could also manage release of the bombs as long as the controls had been switched over from the forward compartment. To aid the photo-navigator in guiding the aircraft to its target there was an auto pilot steering adapter available for use. When engaged this unit connected to the CP-22/APA-44 radar navigational computer. Once control had been transferred from the pilot to the photo- navigator the latter could steer the aircraft manually to its target or should it be necessary via the computer.

The tail gun turret fitted to the RB-45C housed a pair of 0.50 inch machine guns each having 400 rounds of ammunition. Each gun is equipped with a booster unit that automatically feeds rounds to each gun when the trigger is pressed. To ensure that the weapons can be fired under all conditions each gun was fitted with an electrical heater. Sighting of the guns was courtesy of an N-8A non-computing reflex type gun sight which projected a theoretical position on the target approaching the aircraft. Unlike previous bomber weaponry those fitted to the B-45 series of aircraft were not accessible in flight therefore the guns had to be thoroughly inspected by the gunner before flight. However under operational conditions the guns were normally removed to save weight.

Crew comfort in the RB-45C included both fixed and mobile oxygen systems. Should they be needed a mobile unit was provided at each crew station and could be recharged as needed from connections inserted in the main supply system. Each of the fixed positions has a Type A-14 pressure demand regulator for which a pressure demand mask should be used. Under normal operating conditions the regulators would be set to normal however should there be a problem with the normal air mix the regulators could be switched over to 100% oxygen. To cover radio and radar needs aboard the RB-45C it was fitted with numerous systems. Intercommunication between crew member was handled by the AN/ARC-3 while a radio compass, the AN/ARN-6, was used by both the pilot and photo- navigator. In common with the B-45 the reconnaissance aircraft was also fitted with the RC-103-AN/ARN-5A localiser, the AN/AIC-2A interphone and the RC-193-(A) marker beacon. Radar systems fitted to the RB-45C included the AN/APQ-24

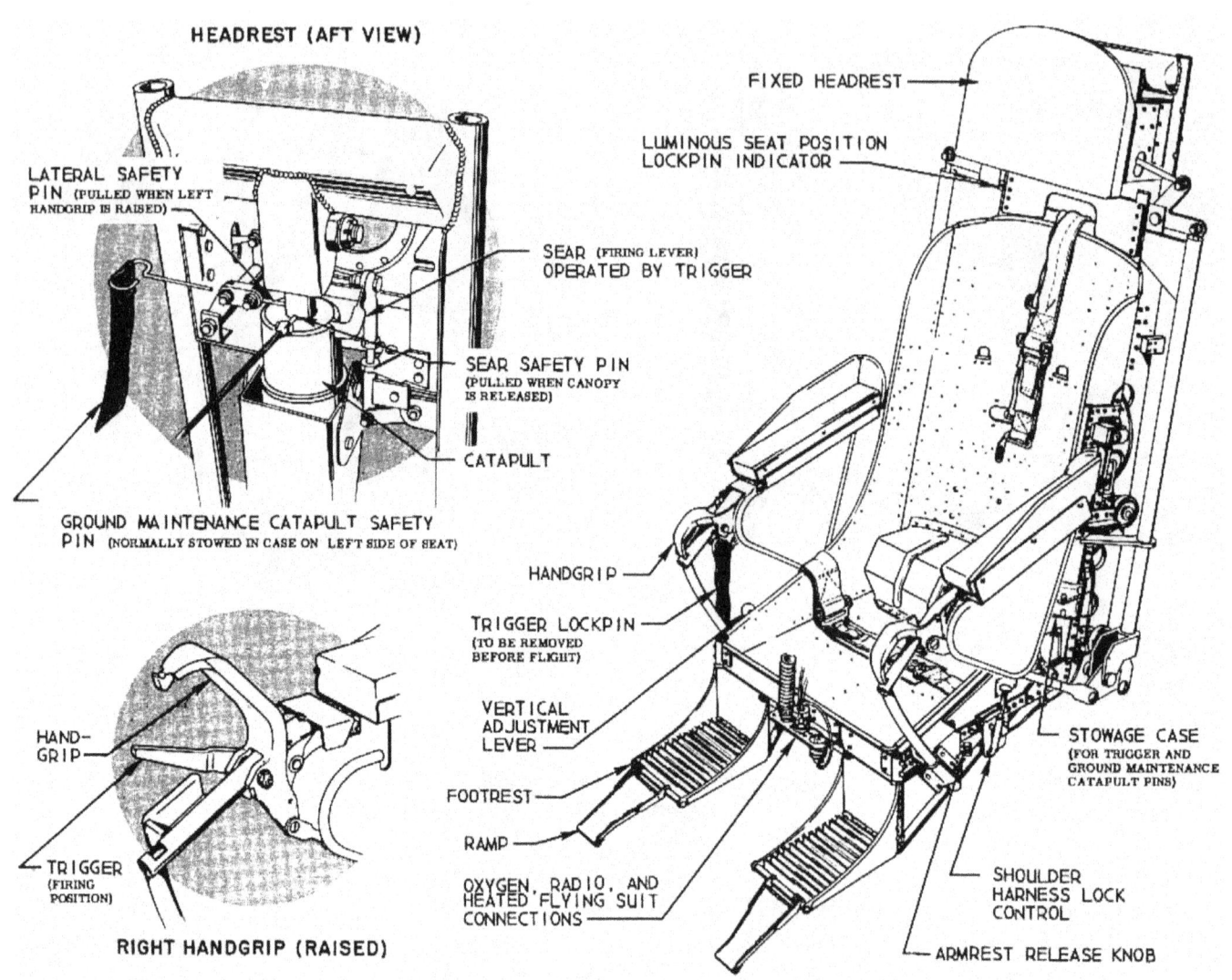

This diagram shows the ejection seats fitted to the RB-45C. As the crew only numbered three only the photo navigator had to bail out.

primary radar, the AN/APN-9 LORAN, AN/APN-3 SHORAN, AN/ APA-54 for navigation, the AN/APN-68 transponder that was used in conjunction with the AN/APN-2B or 12 for use in air refuelling. The final two systems fitted to the aircraft were the AN/APX-6 IFF, the SCR-718C air to ground altitude indicator.

Aircraft Lighting

The exterior lighting fitted to the RB-45C Tornado included the navigation lights mounted on the wingtips and tail all of which could be used for signalling purposes. When the wingtip tanks were fitted the navigation lights were mounted on the tanks. Further lights are mounted on the fuselage on the top with a further two underneath, all could be utilised for signalling using a code selector switch. The aircraft was also fitted with formation lights there being three on top of fuselage while three each were fitted on top of the wing. A landing light was installed in the forward face of the left hand engine nacelle while the taxi light was mounted on the nose wheel leg.

Internal lightning was positioned at the crew panels while a pair of two movable cockpit lights were located at all crew stations. To assist the crew in moving around the forward fuselage
there was a light fitted in the access passage way. Other crew lights were fitted at the photo- navigators station and over the standby compass all having dimmer controls to manage the intensity of the light. Further lights were installed under domes in the aft camera bay while similar lighting was installed in the bomb bays. A light was also installed in the nose wheel bay, this was viewable through a small window in the cockpit floor that allowed the crew to confirm that the nose leg was down and locked.

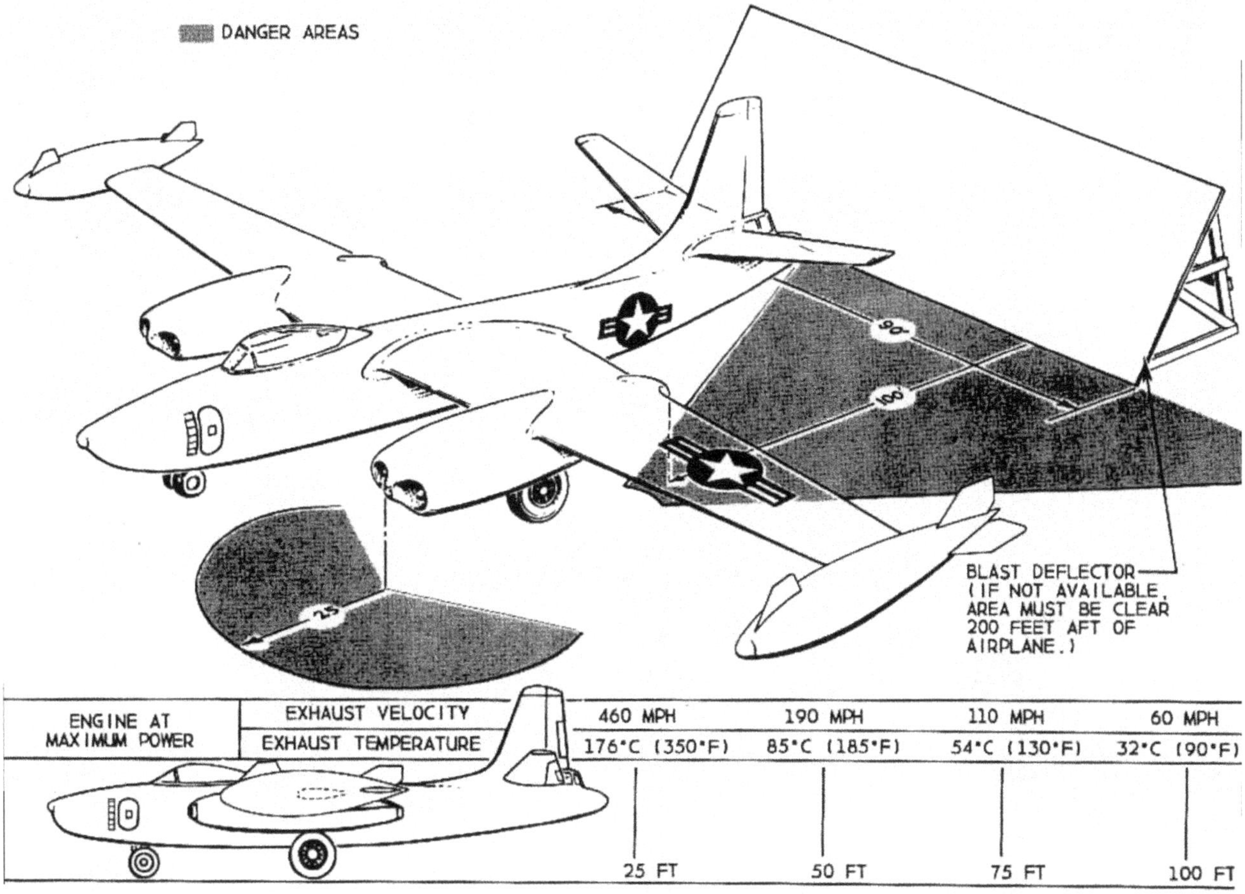

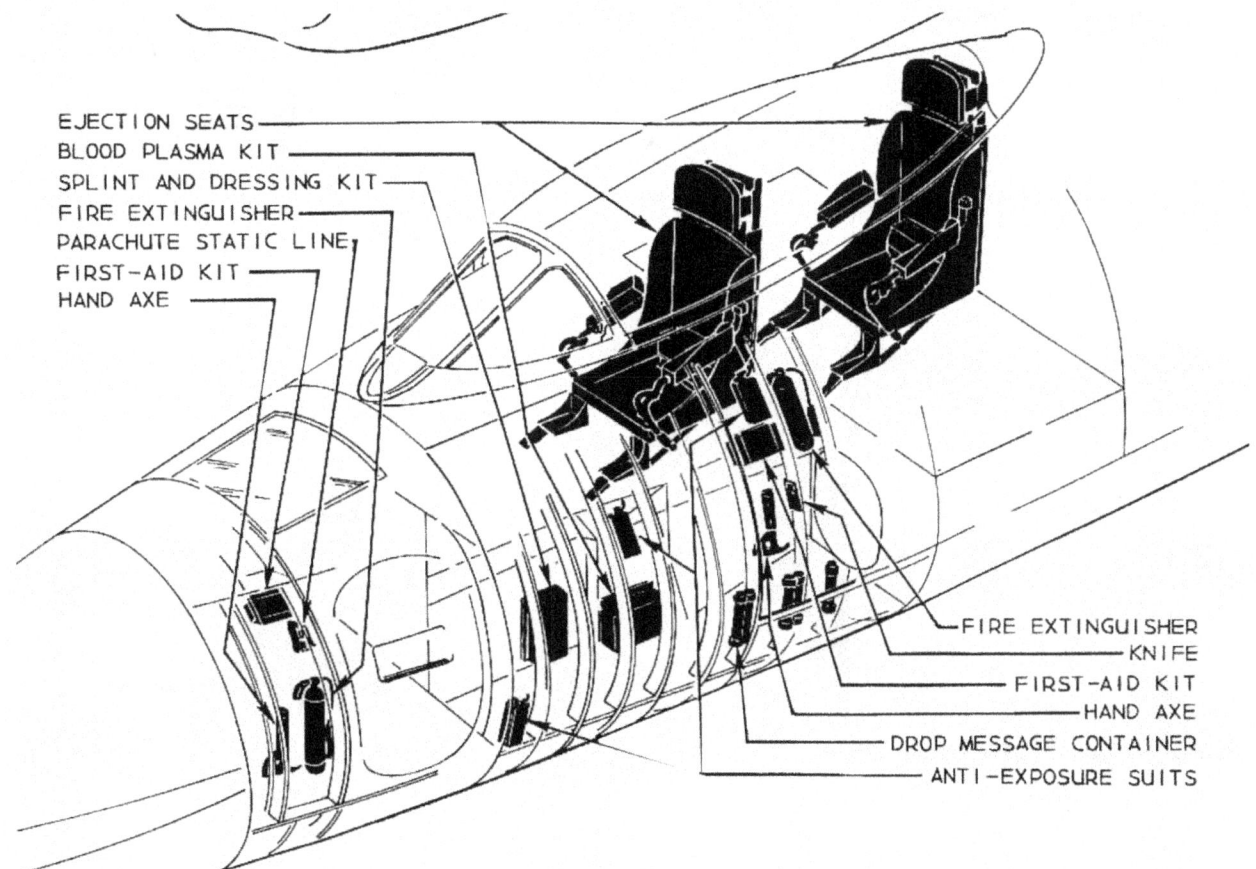

These diagrams show the engine danger areas and the location of the emergency equipment carried in the nose of the RB-45C.

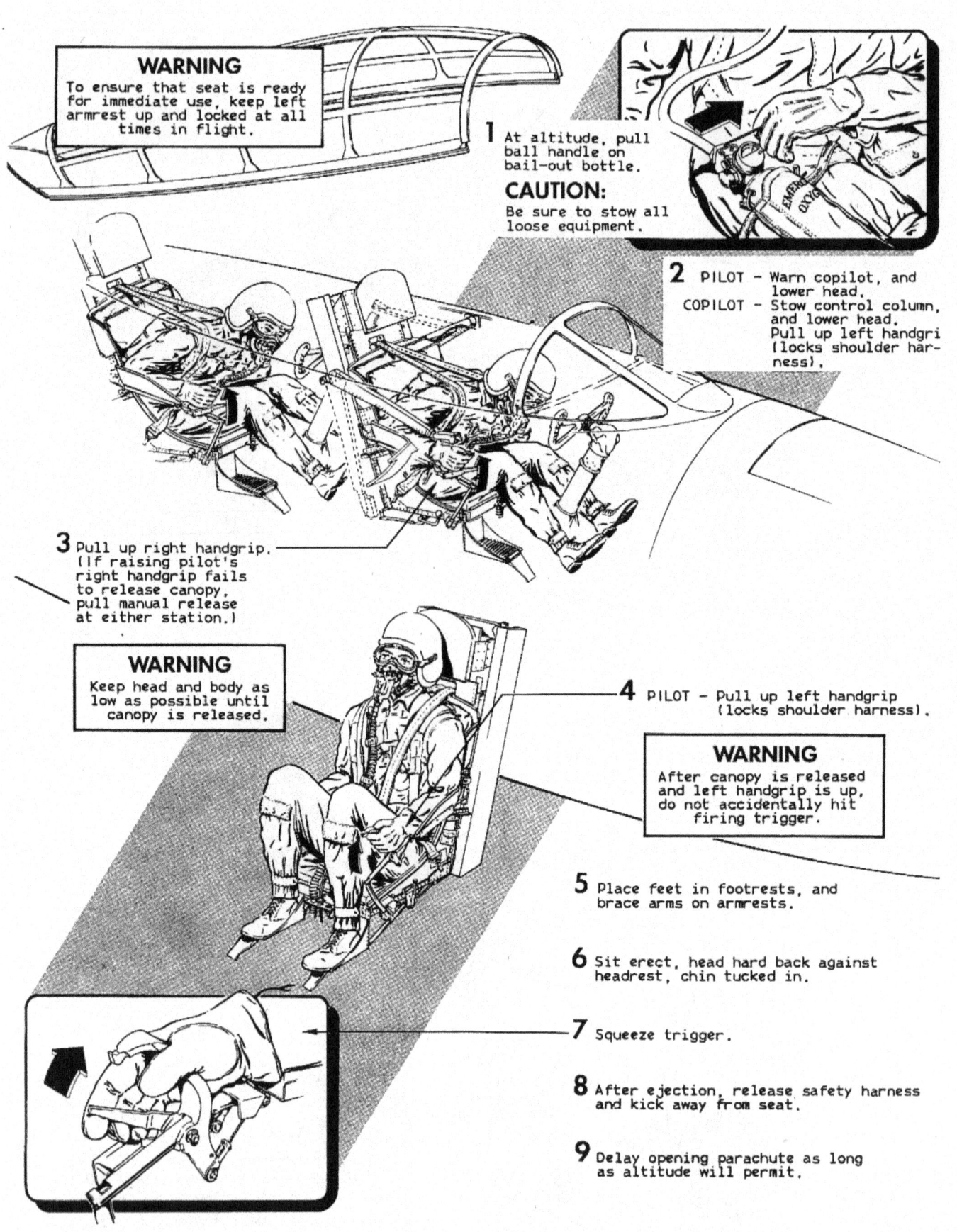

This diagram illustrates the sequence of ejection for the pilot and co-pilot, note that the canopy now features the heavy framing introduced in late build bomber versions.

B-45C 48-001 was retained by North American for trials use although it was later lost in an accident.

NAA B-45/RB-45 TORNADO - CHAPTER FIVE
B-45 TORNADO OPERATIONS AND DEPLOYMENTS

The first operational unit to receive the B-45A was the 47th Bombardment Wing (Light) which was originally based at Biggs AFB, Texas, where it had operated the Douglas A-26 Invader. As Biggs AFB was at an altitude of 3,946 feet and the performance of the early B-45 aircraft was lower than expected it was decided to transfer the wing to Barksdale AFB. Biggs AFB would eventually receive a complement of B-45's when some were transferred there to undertake target towing duties with the 1st Target Towing Squadron. Although suffering from marginal performance these early build aircraft allowed Tactical Air Command to develop the tactics necessary to deliver both high explosive and nuclear ordnance. The 47th BW crews found their new bombers an improvement on their earlier piston powered A-26's even so the aircraft had a few idiosyncrasies of its own. One of the most serious was the failure of the bombardiers compartment glazing. The first occurrence of this was in March 1949 when Colonel Willis Chapman, the commanding officer of the wing, was ferrying an aircraft from the manufacturers to Barksdale AFB. At 30,000 feet there was a failure of the glazing which resulted in complete depressurisation of the complete nose section. Further incidents would result in North American undertaking modification work that increased the Plexiglas sections from three to four. This increase in strength cured the nose glazing failure problems.

Having worked up with a handful of B-45-A-1 machines the 47th BW would receive the far more capable B-45-A-5 models. Eventually the wing received a rotating complement of aircraft that allowed the three squadrons a maximum of fifty aircraft in service out of a total of 96 aircraft. The budgetary axe would start to swing in October 1949 which resulted in the 47th BW being disbanded although two units, the 84th and 85th Bombardment Squadrons, were moved to the 363rd Reconnaissance Wing at Langley AFB, Virginia. These units retained the late build B-45's while the early build aircraft

B-45A-5 47-039 was operated by the 47th Bomb Group and would be lost in a crash in August 1953.

Seen when based in Britain is B-45A-5 47-046 of the 47th Bomb Wing. This was one of the aircraft whose original glazed nose was replaced by a solid cover.

were assigned to secondary duties. While many were assigned to target towing and test duties a handful were given the Backbreaker modifications. This allowed them to be utilised in the testing of nuclear weapons, the first drop was undertaken on 5 November 1951 utilising a 31 Kt weapon this trial being designated Buster Test Easy. The second test was undertaken on 1 May 1952 utilising a 14 Kt weapon this trial being designated Tumbler Snapper Test Dog. The warheads fitted to the test bomb were the Mark 7's intended to arm the Thor ICBM, both drops being made over the Pacific. After these trials the weapons drops were undertaken using Boeing B-47 and B-52 bombers. The National Advisory Committee on Aeronautics, NACA, the precursor to NASA also utilised an early B-45A this being 47-021 that was registered as NACA-121 by this organisation. Operated from Langley this machine was lost in an accident on 14 August 1952 the accident causing the death of test pilot Herbert H Hoover who had managed to eject safely only to strike a part of the structure as he departed, the co-pilot was more fortunate as his seat lifted him clear of the doomed machine.

The 47th Bombardment Wing was reactivated on 12 March 1951 at Langley AFB, Virginia, where the 84th and 85th Bomb Squadrons rejoined. Both units resumed training in both the conventional and nuclear roles. Once re-established the 47th Wing was assigned to Tactical Air Command being redesignated as a Bomb Wing (Tactical) in the process. Although the 47th Wing was undertaking its training the USAF was unsure about the units future usage therefore it was decided to transfer the wing to Europe where it would act in the tactical nuclear weapons delivery role. The chosen base was RAF Sculthorpe where the wing arrived on 1 June 1952. Initially the wing consisted of two squadron the 84th and 85th with a third unit, the 86th BS, being formed on 23 March 1953 although this unit was based at Alconbury as there was not enough room at Sculthorpe for the extra aircraft. The role of the bomber wing in Europe was to provide nuclear weapon support to NATO thus the

After service with the 47th BW in Britain 47-047 was flown to Moron AB for use as in fire and rescue practise by the base firemen.

B-45A-5 47-055 eventually ended its days in France for use as a crash rescue trainer, prior to that it had served with the 47th BW in Britain.

Photographed at Langley AFB 47-057 would eventually join the 47th BW in Britain before ending its days as a fire training aircraft in Morocco.

Sporting a 47th emblem on the nose B-45A 47-058 blasts off the runway in a spirited manner. After service with the 47th BW in Britain the aircraft was despatched to Greenham Common for rescue training purposes.

wing was attached to the 3rd Air Force, USAF, as part of the 49th Air Division. The strength of the 47th Bomb Wing was increased by the addition of the 19th Tactical Reconnaissance Squadron and its RB-45C's although this unit was only on detachment from the 363rd TRW. The 19th TRS was also based at Alconbury alongside the 86th Bomb Squadron. The tactical component would remain in service until the start of 1958 when withdrawals began. As it was not cost effective to return the aircraft to the United States the decision was taken to disperse the fleet around various bases in Europe thus various fighter bases in Britain, France, Spain and Libya would receive redundant bombers that would become the playthings of the base fire services.

Prior to their aircraft meeting a fiery end or the scrapmans axe the B-45's of the 47th Bomb Wing spent much of their time undertaking simulated nuclear training missions against targets throughout Europe all being flown by single aircraft. Most would last for three hours before the aircraft returned to Sculthorpe. Some missions were also undertaken from USAF bases in Libya where many would end their days.

Given their tactical role the wings aircraft kept a very low profile during operations except for those crews that decided that Sculthorpe and the local population would appreciate a high speed low level flypast. Throughout their tenure in East Anglia accidents concerning the B-45 were few however in June 1958 a US Airman decided to appropriate one of the wings bombers for a flight. Unfortunately for the would be pilot his knowledge of aircraft handling was at best sketchy thus he would lose control soon after take off the aircraft crashing on the main railway line near Huntingdon. Little else would disturb the inhabitants of RAF Sculthorpe although the 86th BS housed at Alconbury was forced to move to Molesworth in mid 1956 while urgent maintenance work was undertaken at their home base. Eventually both the bomber and reconnaissance versions of the Tornado would be replaced by the Douglas B/RB-66 Destroyer.

Of those aircraft that remained in America many would become test beds for various experiments centred around the development of various jet engines while others would be fitted with the equipment to tow the Chance Vought target glider. Redesignated

The North American flightline could be a busy place as this view shows. Here B-45A 47-062 sits alongside an F-86 from the same manufacturer while other B-45's undergo pre flight checks. The nearest machine has flap set up gauges on its upper wing.

Photographed while staging through Goose Bay, Canada, the group of B-45's is en route to Britain to join the 47th BW at Sculthorpe.

B-45A 47-073 is seen here taking off on a post modification test flight after the solid nose modification had been applied. It would return to the 47th BW before flying to Morocco for rescue training usage.

Sporting the markings of the 85th BS/47th BW is 47-078 as it takes off using a water methanol mix to boost engine performance. This aircraft was lost after a fire in the air in March 1953.

Photographed while still based at Langley AFB is this group of B-45's belonging to the 47th BW. In this view the rear gunners position is clearly shown. Visible is the remotely operated gun turret, minus guns, plus the sighting mechanism in its clear dome. Also shown is the rear escape hatch and deflector panels.

TB-45A the converted aircraft served with target towing units before being retired in 1960. Other obsolescent aircraft were converted to DB-45A standard and were used in the drone director role. Although North American Aviation were disappointed with the USAF reaction to the B-45 they did attempt to sell further aircraft to the service. The first was the B-45B which featured engines of increased thrust, improved radar systems plus increased range. After this was turned down the company attempted to interest the service in a far more radical concept this being a pilotless guided drone that was intended for use as long range guided bomb.

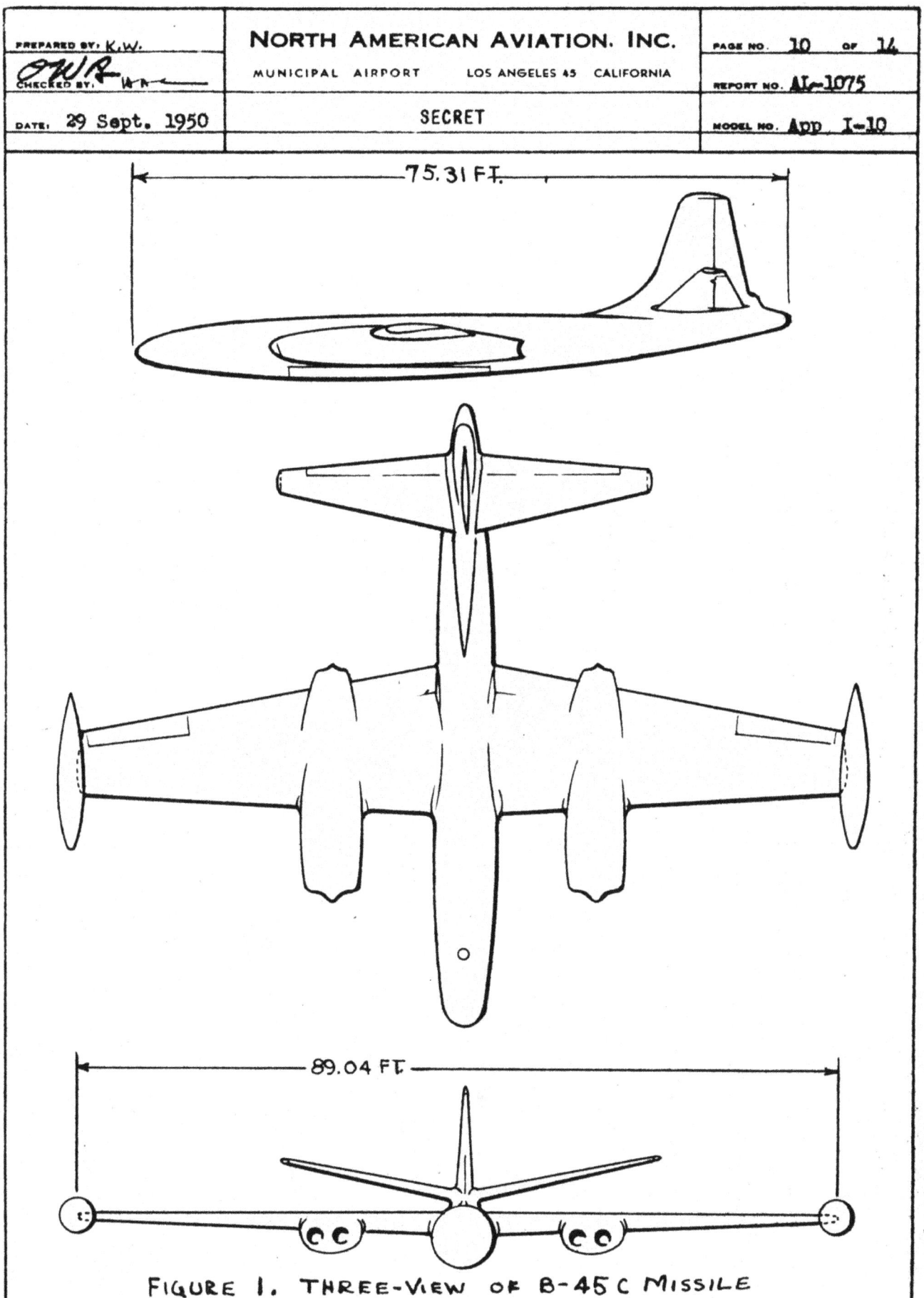

This diagram prepared by NAA shows the proposed B-45C missile version of the bomber.

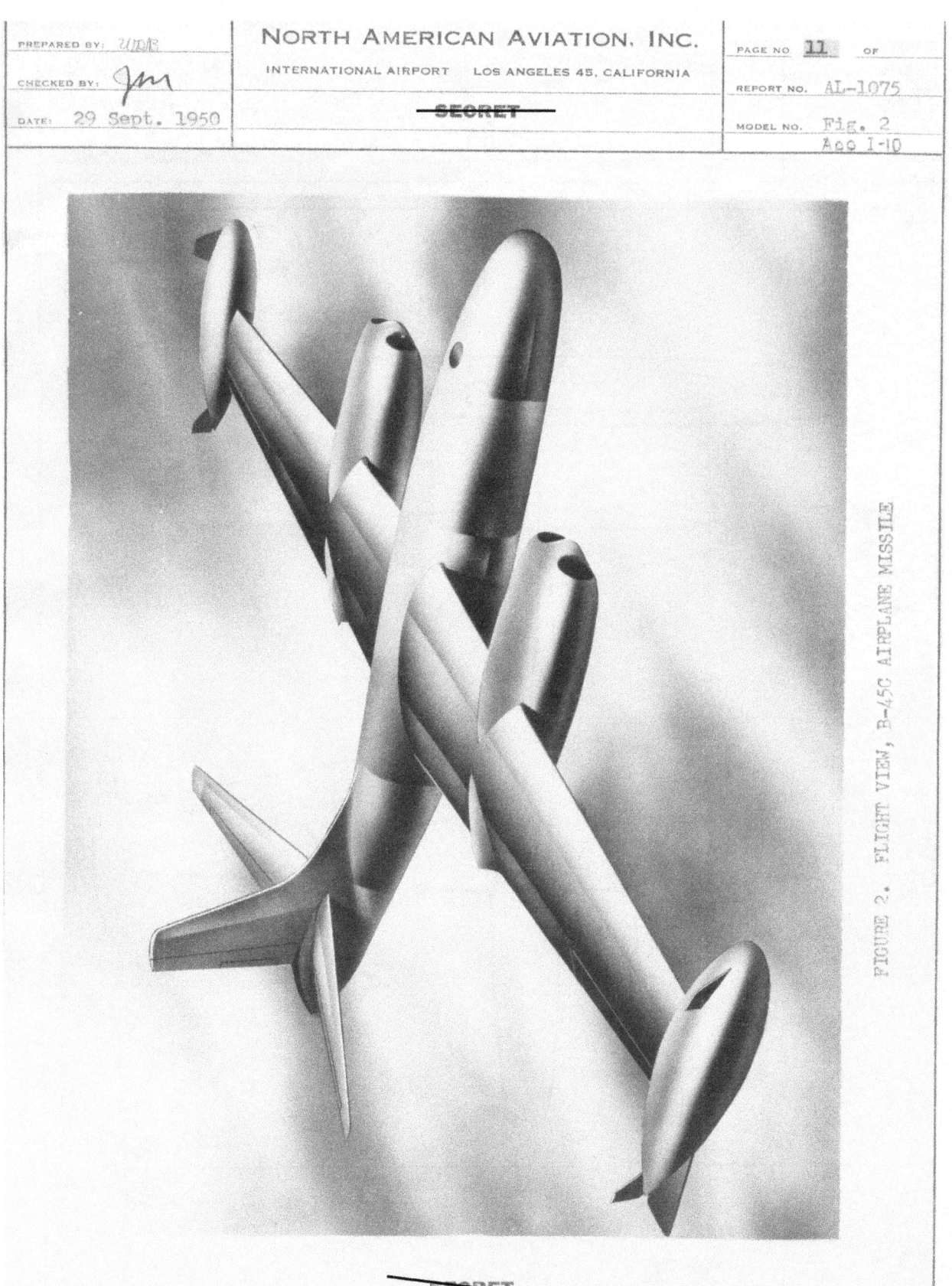

This is an artists impression of the B-45 missile. USAF had no use for such a weapon thus it remained a drawing board exercise only.

Being prepared for departure on the ground at Langley AFB this group of B-45's would stage via Goose Bay amongst other stops on their way to Britain.

One of the stars of the show at a British air display is B-45A 47-083 of the 47th BW. This machine would be written off after crashing in September 1957.

Allocated to the 47th BW at Sculthorpe B-45A 47-087 would finally end its days in Spain as a firemans plaything.

47-080 was assigned to the 84th BS/47th BW when photographed. Of note is the solid nose and the engine blanks to keep unwanted out of the engines. This B-45 was lost after an engine fire in the air in May 1953.

B-45A 47-095 was assigned to the 47th BW at Sculthorpe when photographed. It would end its days in France as rescue trainer.

B-45C 48-001 was retained by the manufacturers for testing and clearance use. This version frequently flew with wing tip tanks fitted.

B-45C 48-005 was bailed to Northrop Aircraft as an EDB-45C drone control aircraft thus it would never enter USAF service.

B-45C 48-010 would spend much of its working life as an EB-45C test and trials aircraft. It is currently on display in the National Museum of the USAF at Wright-Patterson AFB.

With NAA engineers attending to some final details RB-45C 48-011 would be cleared for service use with the 19th SRS.

NAA B-45/RB-45 TORNADO- CHAPTER SIX
RB-45C TORNADO -OPERATIONS AND DEPLOYMENTS

The first RB-45C, 48-011, undertook its maiden flight in April 1950 with deliveries of the production run being made to Lockbourne AFB to the 91st SRW later that year. The RB-45C differed from the bomber versions in that it lacked the tail guns and carried a semi permanent fuel tank in the rear bomb bay although the forward bomb bay was capable of carrying twenty five M-122 photo flash bombs. In this form the Tornado weighed in at 48,000 lbs empty and 120,000 lbs fully laden while top speed was 579 mph at sea level. Maximum altitude was 45,000 feet while unrefuelled range was 1,910 miles.

It would be the RB-45C that would be the most successful of the Tornado versions both in Korea and during its operations from Britain. The primary operator for the RB-45C fleet was the 91st SRW that comprised of three units these being the 322nd, 323rd and 324th Strategic Reconnaissance Squadrons which utilised all of the 33 RB-45C's built for the USAF. The 322nd SRS was allocated to plotting the target tracks for the Bomarc missile while the other two squadrons undertook all the other duties. When the North Korean forces moved over the 38th parallel to begin their invasion of the south on 25 June 1950 the reconnaissance assets available to the USAF in the far east were limited. Originally the 91st SRW sent a detachment of Boeing RB-29 Superfortresses to undertake the mission however their slow speed made them vulnerable to anti aircraft fire and North Korean air force fighters. To counter this USAF proposed to assign jet reconnaissance aircraft to the theatre. The involvement of the RB-45C in the Korean conflict would begin in September 1950 when three machines were flown to Yokota Air Base, Japan, using flight refuelling to reach their destinations although one machine was badly damaged by fire during a refuelling stop at Hawaii. Once in theatre the two remaining aircraft formed Detachment 'A' of the 91st SRW. While the RB-45C was the fastest and best equipped reconnaissance platform available it was not invulnerable. This was graphically revealed on 4 December 1950 when an RB-45C piloted by Captain Charles E McDonough with Colonel James Lovell, Pentagon

Surrounded by a crowd of interested USAF personnel is RB-45C 48-012 that was allocated to the 19th SRS/ 47th BW based at Alconbury.

intel officer, Captain JE Young, co-pilot plus Lt JJ Picucci was shot down by a MiG 15 fighter. It would appear that the lack of tail guns aboard the aircraft seriously reduced the crews chances of survival. While most of the crew are reported to have perished it would appear that Captain McDonough managed to survive and was held by Soviet intelligence for a period afterwards although no word of his fate was ever released. As well as undertaking missions over Korea the RB-45C detachment also flew missions over China to monitor supply shipments and over the Russian post at Vladivostok for the same purpose. The permissions to overfly Russia were given in October 1950 and it would appear that Colonel Lovell was aboard to supervise the first of these spy flights. To replace the missing RB-45C the 91st SRW would despatch a replacement aircraft on 29 July 1952. Piloted by Major Louis Carrington the aircraft, 48-042 'No Sweat', was flown non stop from Elmendorf AFB to Yokota AB in Japan non-stop using aerial refuelling over the whole 4,000 mile flight. The crews reward for this record breaking flight was the Mackay Trophy.

Outside of these record breaking flights the 91st SRW undertook reconnaissance missions over North Korean territory and the various islands held by the communists one of which was over the island of Karafuto, Sakhalin Island, where it was reported that the Soviets had constructed an extensive underground facility and missile launching facilities. Designated Project 51 the RB-45C's of the 91st SRW departed from Yokota AB to undertake overflights over this island plus the Murmansk-Kola inlet. During these flights the KB-29 tanker detachment from the 91st SRW provided refuelling support for the RB-45C's on both the inbound and outbound legs. This service began not long after the arrival of the aircraft in theatre on 14 July 1951. Using the air refuelling option allowed the reconnaissance crews to undertake their overflights at the highest possible speed thus they had the fuel allowance available to undertake evasion manoeuvres should enemy fighters try to intercept. It would be the appearance of the MiG 15 jet fighter that would change the scenario. The earlier Yak9 piston fighters had been easy enough to evade however the MiG 15 was a different prospect entirely. The first

Posed in front of RB-45C 48-013 is Major Louis Carrington and his crew celebrating their record breaking flight although their aircraft was 48-042.

evidence of the MiG's ability to hit the Tornado reconnaissance flights occurred on 4 December 1950 when 48-015 was shot down near the Yalu River, two of the crew died while two others were captured, of those one was hung while the final member died during interrogation. Eventually aircraft and crews from all three squadrons from the 91st SRW were made available to continue the reconnaissance overflights. Further evidence of the MiG's determination to shoot down an RB-45C took place on 9 April 1951 when four attempted to intercept a reconnaissance flight. Fortunately the skills of the pilots and the inability of the MiG pilots to hit a barn door saw the RB-45C run for home undamaged. Another interception on 9 November saw nine MiG's try to shoot down another RB-45C however the pilot again managed to outfly the opposition and return to base unscathed. Theatre command were rightly concerned about the vulnerability of the RB-45C to interception by jet fighters therefore orders were issued that restricted the RB-45C from operating over known heavily defended areas.

This peaceful existence lasted until January 1952 when the RB-45C crews were briefed to undertake night reconnaissance missions. However this was not all plain sailing as opening the front bomb bay to drop photo flash bombs was causing unacceptable turbulence. Even so the 91st crews persevered with their task. One of the first changes applied to some of the detachments aircraft was to paint them in overall black. The first aircraft so finished was 48-027 whose crew was briefed to undertake a pre bombing mission reconnaissance for the B-29 force over the Yalu River area. This zone was known to be well defended by anti aircraft guns and batteries of searchlights plus guidance radar. The need for a change in colour was the ease with which the RB-45C's were being tracked at night, as soon as the searchlights had locked on the aircraft in the cone it was vulnerable to both anti aircraft fire or patrolling MiG fighters as pinned by the lights the aircraft literally glittered. Prior to an active mission being undertaken an unpainted aircraft flew test sorties over Japan in late 1952 where the searchlight batteries of the 507th AA Searchlight Battalion would attempt to intercept it. During all these flights the searchlight operators would quickly pick up on the aircraft's contrails and track them forward to the

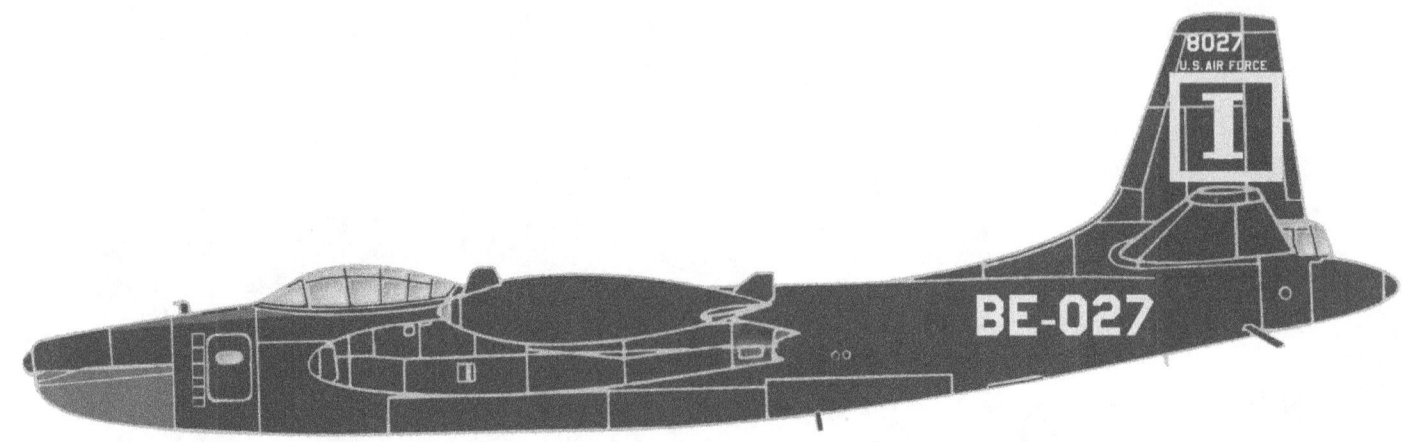

To reduce the chance of interception while undertaking missions over Korea some of the RB-45C's were painted black overall. This change in finish increased their survival chances during these hazardous missions.

aircraft, bearing in mind that this aircraft was travelling at nearly 600 mph at high altitude the results were disheartening. Using the black painted aircraft tracking and intercepting the incoming RB-45C was far more difficult while the Lockheed F-94 Starfire launched to make a practise interception was unable to see the aircraft until closing to within 200 yards of it. Outside of the chance of MiG's shooting down the RB-45's there was also the danger of losses from other causes. An example of these non-combat losses was that of 48-016 which blew its number three engine which also resulted in the loss of No.4 engine. The pilot made strenuous efforts to get the aircraft to a reasonable height at which point the photo-navigator bailed out and both pilots ejected safely.

Pleased with the trial results the 91st SRW were determined to take their black aircraft to a North Korean hot spot. Departing Yokota AB after lifting off at 160 knots the aircraft would retract its undercarriage prior to beginning its climb to height. Once at 500 feet the flaps were retracted and the RB-45 continued its climb to altitude. Even as the RB-45 was taking off so tanker support was moving into position while a search and rescue aircraft was launched to cover the Sea of Japan area. Not only was the rescue aircraft there for the crews benefit its secondary task was to ensure that the RB-45C was totally destroyed as each airframe contained highly secret reconnaissance equipment. As the RB-45C approached the Korean coast the tail guns were armed, external lighting was switched off, the cockpit lights were dimmed and the IFF setting was confirmed. The tail guns were purely for decoy purposes as one was set 10 degrees up while the other was set at 45 degrees down, firing was courtesy of a switch at the pilots position. Now in silent running mode at 35,000 feet the aircraft crossed the coast near Wonsam harbour and changed course towards the designated target. At the initial point just short of the target the pilot started to maintain a straight and level course, this would be the vulnerable point in the flight as the searchlights would be able to lock on without problem. However with the black painted aircraft the North Korean searchlight batteries had problems locking onto the RB-45 as the beams kept sweeping past the aircraft on each pass. Eventually the crew had collected the required infra red and radar data for the forthcoming mission thus they were able to begin their journey home. As they departed the area it was reported that MiG fighters were departing the nearest airfield to intercept. Fortunately there was a reported tail wind at altitude that night thus the aircraft was able to outrun the fighters with ease. As with all such flights under the threat of fighter attack a flight of F-86 Sabres was despatched from Kimpo AB to provide escort. As the flight approached the area where the US Navy assumed responsibility the Sabres would break away to be replaced by Grumman Cougars courtesy of the 7th Fleet. As the RB-45C cleared the furthest point

48-019 was assigned to the 19th SRS/47th BW at Alconbury when photographed. The aircraft was withdrawn from use in August 1957.

RB-45C 48-021 was lost in a take off accident in June 1951 while departing from Alconbury. While based in Britain the aircraft was on the strength of the 19th SRS/ 47th BW.

This portrait has captured RB-45C 48-024 during a test flight minus its wing tip tanks. After entering service the aircraft served with the 323rd SRS/91st SRW.

The 91st SRW also used RB-45C 48-027. Here the reconnaissance aircraft stands alongside other aircraft from the same unit.

After a period with the manufacturers RB-45C 48-031 was assigned to the 91st SRW. Here it wears the square I fin marking and red waist band.

that the North Korean forces were known to operate at the naval fighters were cleared to return to their carrier leaving the Tornado to continue its flight alone. Close to Japan the RB-45C contacted local control and prepared to begin its approach to Yokota. Prior to the days of TACAN or DME the RB-45 had to rely on the AN/ARN-6 low frequency radio compass to steer its course home. This unit operated in the frequency range from 100 to 1,750 kilocycles and was the primary instrument used for let downs. Should there be a problem with the AN/ARN-6 the photo navigator could operate his APN-24 radar plus the ILS system to guide the aircraft down ,or as a final backup, Ground Controlled Approach, GCA, could be utilised. Having made a safe landing at base all of the exposed film would be unloaded and passed to the Reconnaissance Tech to process and pass to the Intelligence Branch for evaluation. This first mission proved that black painted RB-45C's were capable of operating in hostile airspace therefore the type was returned to full active duties.

Operation Ju-Jitsu

Possibly one of the most important tasks carried out by the RB-45C force based in Britain was that of reconnaissance over Russia and its satellites for the bombers of Strategic Air Command. It was for the benefit of the SAC radar navigators that the gathering of such information was needed as flying at high altitudes the SAC bombers radar's could easily pick out the major geographic features and conurbation's however prime military targets such as missile complexes and airfields were not so noticeable especially in bad weather. The answer was to obtain as much reconnaissance data as possible so that target and track maps could be prepared as accurately as possible. Seen as a vital component by the head of SAC, General Curtis LeMay, the use of USAF aircraft for such tasks had been banned by the Truman administration in 1951 much to the chagrin of SAC. Tactical Air Command were also annoyed by the lack of this information as the B-45's based in Britain would also benefit from this intelligence. The answer was a case of mild deception on the behalf of USAF whose response was to ask their counterparts in the Royal Air Force for their assistance. The plan would involve the RAF providing the crews while USAF would provide suitably repainted RB-45C's, both sides would then benefit from the information gathered.

The unit chosen to undertake these missions was the 91st SRW based at Sculthorpe. Prior to the extra tasking the 91st had been fully engaged in undertaking daylight photographic sorties over western Europe using Boeing KB-29P in flight refuelling tankers to extend their mission time to an average of eleven hours. During this missions the crews were instructed to keep their distance from the Soviet bloc border as the airfields in that zone were well stacked with MiG's and the anti aircraft missile defence was improving in capability and reliability. The RAF contingent consisted of three crews, each comprising a pilot, co-pilot and photo-navigator, plus a doctor to monitor the crews health throughout this period. Selected to lead this detachment ,also known as the Special Duties Flight, was Sqdn Ldr Mick Martin who had achieved fame during WW2 during the Dambuster raids. Unfortunately Sqdn Ldr Martin would fail the medical needed to clear him for high altitude flying as he was found to be suffering from a lung condition. His replacement was Sqdn Ldr John Crampton who would assume command in July 1951 after briefing at Bomber Command. The crew members selected for this flight were drawn from the Lincoln and B-29 Washington squadrons. Once all the various selected crews had been gathered together they were despatched to Barksdale AFB , Louisiana, in September 1951. From Barksdale the crews then transferred to Langley AFB, Virginia, to continue their training , later moving to Lockbourne AFB, Ohio, for completion. During this period the pilots learned to fly their new mounts while the navigators learned how to operate the radar and associated systems all coming together to undertake training missions using the RB-45C's based in the United States. At the completion of their training period the RAF crews returned to Britain where they took up quarters at RAF Sculthorpe. Once acclimatised the crews began day and night overflights of Europe to reinforce their training in America. It was during these UK training flights that one pilot executed a heavy landing that was severe enough to write off the aircraft. While the crew escaped unscathed General LeMay requested an interview with the pilot. The miscreant was flown to the United States where the General left him in no doubt that he was not impressed by people who broke his aeroplanes. The

Being refuelled by a Boeing KB-29 also allocated to the 91st SRW is RB-45C 48-031. Both are resplendent in the units markings.

Prior to being operated by the 19th SRS/ 47th BW from Alconbury RB-45C 48-033 was utilised in JATO unit trials. Here it departs Griffis AFB with both units developing full power. As was common with this version the tail gun turret is faired over to save weight.

pilot was returned to Britain where he was returned to his original unit being replaced a better qualified individual. During these flights most of the crews were under the impression that they were either evaluating the RB-45C, unlikely as the EE Co Canberra was entering service, or that they were determining whether boom or probe refuelling was the better system. Even as these were being undertaken the government of Clement Attlee were unsure whether to allow these proposed flights to take place however a change of government to one led by Winston Churchill changed the British attitude to this operation.

The first flight was undertaken on 21 March 1952 although this was purely a probing flight to see how the Russian forces would react to a jet bomber flying up and down the Berlin corridor at high speed and high altitude given the sensitivity of this particular piece of airspace. Having survived unscathed the three crews waited for their first operational mission. On 16 April 1952 the flights leaders went to Bomber Command for a briefing. Their given tasks involved each crew flying their aircraft along three separate routes. The first involved departing Britain , flying over Germany over to the Baltic States, the second also involved flying over Germany although the navigation track would lead the aircraft south of Moscow while the third aircraft was scheduled to aim for the central region of Russia before turning south to reconnoitre some of the industrial sites in southern Ukraine. During the crew brief they were given three separate briefings, one was the true briefing, the second was for general consumption for those at Sculthorpe while the final was intended for Russian ears in case any of the aircraft were shot down. Backing up the briefings a complete set of fake maps and notes was given to each crew.

Over the night of 17-18 April the three assigned aircraft plus the spare machine were pulled out of the hangars at Sculthorpe and moved to the flight line. Whilst sat in the hangar the aircraft had all their USAF markings removed these being replaced by RAF markings although no British serial numbers were assigned. This was intended to create chaos in the Soviet intelligence community as the USAF could deny the aircraft belonged to them and it was highly likely that the Russians were fully aware that the RAF had no RB-45C's on inventory. After take off the three RB-45's were air refuelled by USAF KB-29 tankers before proceeding on their allotted tasks. After completing their missions all three aircraft returned safely having spent approximately 10.5 hours each airborne although only the aircraft piloted

RB-45C 48-036 forms the backdrop as a group of dignitaries undertake an inspection of the 91st SRG. 48-036 later served in Britain with the 19th SRS.

Destined to serve with the manufacturers amongst other user for trials work RB-45C 48-037 was finally retired to Norton AFB in December 1957.

The 91st SRG had its own dedicated refuelling unit, the 91st ARS which flew the Boeing KB-29 tanker from Lockbourne AFB. Here RB-45C 48-038 takes fuel from 483927.

by Sqdn Leader Crampton managed to land at Sculthorpe through a break in the clouds. Of the others that piloted by Flt Lt Blair was forced to divert to Manston as visibility at Sculthorpe had dropped below safe minima while the third machine, piloted by Flt Lt Cremer had landed at Copenhagen due to engine malfunctions caused by icing of the fuel systems, once this was clear the Tornado departed Denmark later making a safe landing at Sculthorpe. Once the aircraft had shut down the reconniassance films were rushed to a waiting Canberra from RAF Wyton who flew the films to the Central Reconnaissance Establishment for processing and interpretation. In recognition of their bravery all the participating aircrew were awarded the Air Force Cross or Medal depending on rank, this medal could be awarded in peacetime as no public citation was required. Having completed their missions successfully Sqdn Ldr Crampton plus another pilot were invited to meet General LeMay at Lockbourne AFB. Their chosen method of transport was an RB-45C that they flew via Goose Bay into the United States. After a period of leave in America the two officers returned to Britain after which the Special Duties Flight was disbanded all crewmen returning to their respective units.

This could have been the end of such overflights however in September 1952 a letter from Sir John Slessor, Chief of the Air Staff, to his counterpart in the USAF ,General Vandenberg, suggested that the RB-45C flights over Soviet held territory be resumed to update the target data and maps. Designated Operation *Ju-Jitsu* the RAF crews would be withdrawn from their normal duties to undertake training for these missions. Once again Sqdn Ldr John Crampton, by now commanding officer of No.101 Squadron flying Canberra's, was designated as commander although there was one change as one of the previous crewmen had been seriously injured in a B-29 Washington crash. Even with these changes the crews still needed their skills updating therefore in October flying training began. Five weeks later the entire training programme was called off for no apparent reason. The entire operation was held in abeyance for fourteen months before *Ju-Jitsu* was resurrected for further training. As with all such operations these detachments to Sculthorpe were put forward as exchange postings however in reality the RAF crews were undergoing extensive training in radar reconnaissance techniques, although when not on operations the RAF crewmen did fly as part of mixed crews in USAF marked aircraft. The aircraft assigned to these missions were drawn from those based at Shaw AFB with the 363rd SRW. Prior to departing the United States all four machines were flown by TAC crews to Wright Patterson AFB for

Climbing into the sky is RB-45C 48-037 assigned to the 91st Strategic Reconnaissance Wing based at Lockbourne AFB. At the completion of its service this aircraft was flown to Norton AFB for disposal.

modifications. These mainly centred around the radar units, these being updated to produce crisper results courtesy of British engineers who supervised the work. As before the briefing laid out three routes similar to those flown before although there was an extra slant to the missions as both the British and Americans were very interested in the reactions of the Soviet Air Forces to aircraft penetrating their airspace without permission. To that end GCHQ based in Cheltenham plus airborne monitoring aircraft supplied by USAF would be monitoring both communications and radar signals in a combined effort to ascertain the Soviet reaction pattern.

On the night of 28-29 April 1954 the three chosen RB-45C's were rolled out of their hangar to be prepared for their flights, however by this time the RB-45C had been transferred en bloc from Strategic Air

During Operation Ju-Jitsu the RB-45C's flown by the RAF crews sported British markings in place of their normal USAF colours. No external serials or other marks were applied although this machine did sport the name 'Foto Genie' under the cockpit.

Command to Tactical Air Command thus General LeMay who had sponsored all the previous missions was no longer directly involved. As before all traces of USAF ownership had been removed to be replaced by their RAF counterparts. The targets chosen for each of the target routes were scattered in such a way that plotting their next position would be difficult. Once airborne the three reconnaissance machines headed for their targets inside Russia undertaking in flight refuelling as needed. Given the almost random tracks of the three aircraft their antics appeared to ignite the whole Soviet Air Defence network. As these missions were flown at night and the MiG's lacked interception radar, vectoring was courtesy of ground control however it was proving impossible for the fighters to find the intruders although the Russian pilots showed much determination even being ordered to ram the interlopers if possible. In areas not covered by fighters the local anti aircraft commanders let their batteries loose in an attempt to down an RB-45C although they were as unsuccessful as their airborne counterparts. The only problem encountered was one aircraft that could not hook up to the tanker as there was a fault with the reconnaissance aircraft's receptacle thus the thirsty RB-45 was forced to land at Furstenfeldenbruck Air Base in Germany. This obviously caused a certain amount of chaos as would be expected when an unannounced aircraft arrives from the Soviet Bloc with an urgent request for fuel in the dead of night. In order to keep the resultant fuss under control the RB-45 was quickly refuelled and sent on its way In contrast to the earlier missions the photographic results were far clearer as Bomber Commands chief scientist, Lew Llewelen had worked miracle's to improve the results. While both sets of RB-45C missions had been successful and were carried out without loss this would be the final set of overflights as the Tornado was heading for obscelesence and the Soviets would make great efforts from that date to introduce improved air defences. This would also mark the end of the RAF involvement with the RB-45C as further operations would come under the control of the 19th Tactical Reconnaissance Squadron that came into existence on 11 May 1954.

The fate of many an NAA Tornado- to lie battered and abused on the side of an airfield somewhere while fire and rescue crews practise their arts. This particular aircraft is 47-056 late of the 47th BW.

Some of the earlier Allison J35 powered B-45A's had second role after their short bomber lives. Their role was to provide high speed target towing facilities to the fighter community. Converted to TB-45A-1 standard 48-018 was operated by the 1st TTS from Biggs AFB.

Tornado Test Beds

The North American B-45 Tornado also saw some use as an engine test bed its large bomb bays could comfortably accommodate an engine and its extension/retraction mechanism. The first such machine was B-45A-5-NA 47-096 that was bailed to the Westinghouse Corporation for flight trials of the J34 engine. While the engine produced adequate performance it was never seen as prime mover finally finding is niche as an auxiliary or boost engine. Also converted for use as a test bed was JB-45C ,48-009, that was assigned to flight trials of the Allison J71. The aircraft was sent to Allison's for conversion at Plant 10 located Weir Cook Airport, Indianapolis this being completed by December 1952. The modification work included fitting a retraction/extension mechanism which allowed the engine to run at full power when fully extended while for take off and landing it was retracted up to the lower fuselage line. After initial flight trials by Allison the Tornado was despatched to Edwards AFB for extensive testing during which the test aircraft was flown to the maximum altitude available to the B-45. After completing its flight trials the Allison J71 was chosen to power the Douglas B-66 Destroyer and the McDonnell F3H-2 Demon fighters. General Electric would be the third manufacturer to utilise the B-45 as a engine test bed this being JRB-45C, 48-017, that would first be used to trial the J79 engine that was later used to power the Convair B-58 Hustler and Lockheed F-104 Starfighter. The aircraft was based at Schenectady, New York, where it was operated by the Flight Test Division of the General Engineering and Consulting Laboratory. The main problem encountered during the flight testing of these various powerplants was the tendency to suffer pitch instability when an installed afterburner was operated although the burner was only operated for short periods of time. After completion of its work for General Electric 48-017 was transferred to Pratt & Whitney for an unspecified task. Eventually laid up due to the lack of spares a strong effort was made to make it flyable again after which it was flown to the Strategic Air Command Museum at Offut AFB, Nebraska, where it arrived in June 1972. Also preserved are B-45A, 47-008, located at Castle AFB and B-45C , 48-010, now on display at the National Museum of the USAF at Wright-

Patterson AFB, Dayton, Ohio, where it sports the markings of the 47th Bomb Wing.

During its short period of service the B-45 Tornado managed some significant firsts that included being the first four jet bomber in USAF service and being the first aircraft to undertake boom flight refuelling as a standard. Outside of these achievements the B-45 was initially an aircraft without a role however a transfer of command and a major modification programme ensured that the aircraft had a future as a tactical nuclear bomber. Its other merit came from the RB-45C reconnaissance version which undertook daring missions over North Korea and European Russia. It is a great shame therefore that this significant aircraft has ended up as America's forgotten bomber.

NAA B-45C Tornado 48-002 was converted to EB-45C standard for use by the manufacturers and other organisations for trials use. It was reported as lost in April 1951 after a landing accident.

By the time B-45C 48-002 rolled off the production line the nose canopy was fitted with a four frames as standard. Here 48-002 awaits its next flight at Edwards AFB.

Operated as a JB-45C 48-009 is seen in flight with a General Electric J79 engine mounted in a pod under the bomb bay. Once started it was quite usual for the bombers own engines to be set to idle while power was supplied by the J79.

When the J79 was in the partially lowered position the bomb doors opened to allow the pod to extend fully after which they closed. The doors were modified to give a close fit around the engine pod when fully deployed.

Currently on display at the Strategic Air Command Museum at Offut AFB is JRB-45C 48-017. Used to test both the J57 and J75 engines this aircraft was finally retired by Pratt & Whitney in 1972.

With a P&W J57 engine mounted on the bomb bay pylon JRB-45C 48-017 poses for the camera. This aircraft was a unique machine as it was the only B-45 to be fitted with airbrakes whose upper line truncates the fuselage star and bar.

Seen before it became a fully fledged engine testbed is JRB-45C 48-017 complete with prominent mounting of unknown purpose under the rear fuselage. Also prominent is the fuel dump above the fairing plus the marking for the flight refuelling receptacle on the upper fuselage.

APPENDIX ONE
NORTH AMERICAN AVIATION B-45A/C and RB-45C
SERIAL NUMBERS AND SHORT HISTORIES

Tail Number	C/N	Model	Operating Units	Remarks
45-59479	130-38391	XB-45	NAA Muroc AFB	Cr 28 Jun 1949-engine failure.
45-59480	130-38392	XB-45	FTD Wright-Patterson	withdrawn from use for spares
45-59481	130-38393	XB-45	FTD Wright-Patterson	withdrawn from use- used as ground trainer
47-001	147-43401	B-45A-1-NA	Test Dept- Muroc AFB	Cr 20 Sep 1948- crew killed
47-002	147-43402	B-45A-1-NA	FTD Wright-Patterson	W/o 6 Oct 1948- mech failure on take off
47-003	147-43403	B-45A-1-NA		withdrawn from use for spares
47-004	147-43404	B-45A-1-NA		withdrawn from use for spares
47-005	147-43405	B-45A-1-NA		withdrawn from use for spares
47-006	147-43406	B-45A-1-NA	1st TargetTow Squadron	Cr 15 Jan 1951 -structural failure
47-007	147-43407	B-45A-1-NA	As TB-45A- 2nd TTS	W/o 15 Jul 1953- ground accident
47-008	147-43408	B-45A-1-NA	To China Lake	Preserved-Castle AFB
47-009	147-43409	B-45A-1-NA	47th Bomb Group	withdrawn from use for spares
47-010	147-43410	B-45A-1-NA	85th BS/ 47th BG	withdrawn from use for spares
47-011	147-43411	B-45A-1-NA	47th Bomb Group	withdrawn from use for spares
47-012	147-43412	B-45A-1-NA	As EB-45A 3077th EG Edwards AFB	W/o 17 Aug 1950- structural failure
47-013	147-43413	B-45A-1-NA	47th Bomb Group	withdrawn from use for spares
47-014	147-43414	B-45A-1-NA	As EB-45A 29th AMS/ 29th AMG	W/o 10 Aug 1951- landing accident
47-015	147-43415	B-45A-1-NA	47th Bomb Group	withdrawn from use for spares
47-016	147-43416	B-45A-1-NA	47th Bomb Group	withdrawn from use for spares
47-017	147-43417	B-45A-1-NA	29th MSU	Cr 21 Dec 1949- landing accident.
47-018	147-43418	B-45A-1-NA	as TB-45A 1st TTS	withdrawn from use for spares
47-019	147-43419	B-45A-1-NA	47th Bomb Group	withdrawn from use for spares
47-020	147-43420	B-45A-1-NA	47th Bomb Group	withdrawn from use for spares
47-021	147-43421	B-45A-1-NA	47th Bomb Group	withdrawn from use for spares
47-022	147-43422	B-45A-1-NA	47th Bomb Group	withdrawn from use for spares
47-023	147-43423	B-45A-5-NA	86th BS/ 47th BG	withdrawn from use for spares
47-024	147-43424	B-45A-5-NA	FTD Wright-Patterson	W/o 21 Mar 1949- mechanical failure
47-025	147-43425	B-45A-5-NA	47th Bomb Group	withdrawn from use for spares
47-026	147-43426	B-45A-5-NA	3200th BS 3200th PTG	W/o 30 Oct 1950-landing accident due to mechanical failure
47-027	147-43427	B-45A-5-NA	85th BS/ 47th BG	Wfu 19 Jun 1958 to RAF Bruntingthorpe-fire service use
47-028	147-43428	B-45A-5-NA	84th BS 363rd TRG	W/o 14 Feb 1950- crash landing after engine failure
47-029	147-43429	B-45A-5-NA	84th BS/ 47th BG	Wfu 8 Apr 1958 to Spangdahlam AB for fire service use
47-030	147-43430	B-45A-5-NA	84th BS/ 47th BW	Wfu 16 Jun 1958-to Alconbury for fire use
47-031	147-43431	B-45A-5-NA	HQ Sdn 3077th EG	W/o 25 Jun 1951 - landing accident after mechanical failure
47-032	147-43432	B-45A-5-NA	84th BS 363rd TRG	W/o 28 May 1950 -crash landed after mechanical failure
47-033	147-43433	B-45A-5-NA	85th BS / 47th BG	W/o 9 Jun 1949- aircraft crashed after mechanical failure
47-034	147-43434	B-45A-5-NA	85th BS 363rd TRG	W/o 7 Jul 1950-crashed due to mech failure
47-035	147-43435	B-45A-5-NA	47th BG	Wfu 19 Jun 1958-to Brize Norton for fire use
47-036	147-43436	B-45A-5-NA	HQ Sdn AFFTC	W/o 4 Apr 1952- taxi accident
47-037	147-43437	B-45A-5-NA	84th BS / 47th BG	W/o 12 Aug 1949 - crash landed after engine failure and fire
47-038	147-43438	B-45A-5-NA	2750th AMG	W/o 23 Mar 1951 ground accident

Tail Number	C/N	Model	Operating Units	Remarks
47-039	147-43439	B-45A-5-NA	84th BS / 47th BG	Cr 19 Aug 1953 - structural failure
47-040	147-43440	B-45A-5-NA	85th BS 363rd TRG	W/o 3 Feb 1950- crash landed after engine failure
47-041	147-43441	B-45A-5-NA	322nd SRS/91st SRG	Cr 21 Mar 1951
47-042	147-43442	B-45A-5-NA	22nd SRS/ 91st SRG	W/o 20 Jun 1951- ground accident after damage by enemy fire
47-043	147-43443	B-45A-5-NA	84th BS/ 47th BG	Wfu 10 Jul 1958-to Chelveston for fire service use
47-044	147-43444	B-45A-5-NA	85th BS / 47th BG	W/o 31 Aug 1949- crashed after engine failure
47-045	147-43445	B-45A-5-NA	85th BS 363rd TRG	Cr 4 Apr 1950- structural failure
47-046	147-43446	B-45A-5-NA	84th BS / 47th BG	W/o 18 Nov 1950- engine fire
47-047	147-43447	B-45A-5-NA	47th BG	Wfu 11 Jun 1958-to Spain for fire service use
47-048	147-43448	B-45A-5-NA	86th BS/ 47th BG	Wfu 11 Jun 1958-to Spain for fire service use
47-049	147-43449	B-45A-5-NA	85th BS / 47th BG	W/o 15 Jan 1951- mechanical failure
47-050	147-43450	B-45A-5-NA	NAA trials a/c	Withdrawn from use 5 Apr 1957
47-051	147-43451	B-45A-5-NA	84th BS 363rd TRG	W/o 22 Nov 1949- mechanical failure
47-052	147-43452	B-45A-5-NA	343rd SRS/91st SRG	W/o 24 Oct 1951- take off accident
47-053	147-43453	B-45A-5-NA	85th BS 363rd TRG	W/o 25 Jan 1950- fire and explosion
47-054	147-43454	B-45A-5-NA	47th BG	Wfu 25 Jun 1958-to France for fire service use
47-055	147-43455	B-45A-5-NA	86th BS/ 47th BG	Wfu 8 Apr 1958- to France for fire service use
47-056	147-43456	B-45A-5-NA	84th BS 363rd TRG	Wfu 1958 -to Alconbury for crash rescue training.
47-057	147-43457	B-45A-5-NA	84th BS/ 47th BS	Wfu 11 June 1958 -to Morocco for fire service use
47-058	147-43458	B-45A-5-NA	84th BS/ 47th BW	Wfu Oct 1958-to Greenham Common for fire use
47-059	147-43459	B-45A-5-NA	86th BS/ 47th BG	Cr 30 Jan 1956
47-060	147-43460	B-45A-5-NA	47th BG	Cr 14 Dec 1952
47-061	147-43461	B-45A-5-NA	84th BS / 47th BG	Cr 25 May 1951- landing accident.
47-062	147-43462	B-45A-5-NA	86th BS/ 47th BG	Withdrawn from use 4 Apr 1958
47-063	147-43463	B-45A-5-NA	47th BG	Wfu- nose to Pima Air Museum
47-064	147-43464	B-45A-5-NA	85th BS/ 47th BG	cr 12 Dec 1951-due to lack of fuel
47-065	147-43465	B-45A-5-NA	85th BS/ 47th BG	Wfu 19 Jun 1958-to Lakenheath for fire service
47-066	147-43466	B-45A-5-NA	85th BS/ 47th BG	Wfu 1 Aug 1958-to Spain for fire service use
47-067	147-43467	B-45A-5-NA	47th BG	Wfu 15 May 1958- to Germany for fire service use
47-068	147-43468	B-45A-5-NA	85th BS/ 47th BG	W/o 21 April 1953- engine fire in the air
47-069	147-43469	B-45A-5-NA	47th BG	Wfu 8 Aug 1958- to Spain for fire service use
47-070	147-43470	B-45A-5-NA	47th BG	Cr Nov 1953
47-071	147-43471	B-45A-5-NA	47th BG	Cr 3 Jun 1957
47-072	147-43472	B-45A-5-NA	47th BG	Cr 14 Mar 1956
47-073	147-43473	B-45A-5-NA	47th BG	Wfu 7 Jul 1958 -to Morocco for fire service use
47-074	147-43474	B-45A-5-NA	47th BG	Wfu 19 May 1958- to Germany for fire use
47-075	147-43475	B-45A-5-NA	47th BG	Withdrawn from use
47-076	147-43476	B-45A-5-NA	47th BG	Wfu Jul 1958 -to Italy for fire service use
47-077	147-43477	B-45A-5-NA	47th BG	Wfu 15 May 1958- to Germany for fire service use
47-078	147-43478	B-45A-5-NA	85th BS/ 47th BG	W/o 9 Mar 1953- fire in the air
47-079	147-43479	B-45A-5-NA	85th BS/ 47th BG	W/o 2 April 1953- engine failure
47-080	147-43480	B-45A-5-NA	84th BS / 47th BG	W/o 11 May 1953- engine fire in the air
47-081	147-43481	B-45A-5-NA	47th BG	Wfu 7 Jul 1958- to Morocco for fire service use
47-082	147-43482	B-45A-5-NA	84th BS/ 47th BW	Wfu 7 Jul 1958- to Morocco for fire service use
47-083	147-43483	B-45A-5-NA	47th BW	Cr 20 Sep 1957
47-084	147-43484	B-45A-5-NA	47th BW	Wfu 26 Jun 1958- to Germany for fire service use
47-085	147-43485	B-45A-5-NA	85th BS/ 47th BG	Withdrawn from use
47-086	147-43486	B-45A-5-NA	47th BW	Wfu and scrap 4 Apr 1958
47-087	147-43487	B-45A-5-NA	47th BW	Wfu 8 Aug 1958- to Spain for fire use
47-088	147-43488	B-45A-5-NA	47th BW	Withdrawn from use
47-089	147-43489	B-45A-5-NA	84th BS/ 47th BW	Wfu 13 May 1958- to France for fire service use
47-090	147-43490	B-45A-5-NA	47th BW	Wfu Aug 1950- to Morocco for fiire service use
47-091	147-43491	B-45A-5-NA	47th BW	Wfu 11 Jul 1958- to France for fire service use
47-092	147-43492	B-45A-5-NA	47th BW	Wfu 9 Apr 1958- to Germany for fire service use
47-093	147-43493	B-45A-5-NA	422nd BS	5 Feb 1953 - take off accident

Tail Number	C/N	Model	Operating Units	Remarks
47-094	147-43494	B-45A-5-NA	84th BS/47th BW	W/o 30 Nov 1951- take off accident
47-095	147-43495	B-45A-5-NA	47th BW	Wfu 8 Apr 1958- to France for fire service use
47-096	147-43496	B-45A-5-NA	47th BW	Withdrawn from use
47-097	147-43497	B-45A-5-NA	NAA	Static test airframe
48-001	153-38477	B-45C-1-NA	North American Flight Test Dept as EB-45C	W/o 28 Sep 1950- structural failure
48-002	153-38478	B-45C-1-NA		W/o 11 Apr 1951- landing accident
48-003	153-38479	B-45C-1-NA	47th BW	Withdrawn from use
48-004	153-38480	B-45C-1-NA	47th BW	Withdrawn from use
48-005	153-38481	B-45C-1-NA	As EDB-45C- Northrop Aircraft	W/o 12 Aug 1953- ground fire
48-006	153-38482	B-45C-1-NA	AWFD	Cr 24 Feb 1950 after fire and explosion
48-007	153-38483	B-45C-1-NA	47th BW	Withdrawn from use
48-008	153-38484	B-45C-1-NA	To JB-45C	Withdrawn from use
48-009	153-38485	B-45C-1-NA	To JB-45C	Withdrawn from use
48-010	153-38486	B-45C-1-NA	AMC as EB-45C	Preserved at NMUSAF W-P AFB
48-011	153-38487	RB-45C-1-NA	19th SRS/47th BW	Wfu 1 Oct 1957
48-012	153-38488	RB-45C-1-NA	19th SRS/ 47th BW	Wfu 2 Oct 1957 -to France for fire service use
48-013	153-38489	RB-45C-1-NA	19th SRS/ 47th BW	Wfu 28 Apr 1958- to Turkey for fire service use
48-014	153-38490	RB-45C-1-NA	19th SRS/ 47th BW	Wfu 28 Apr 1958-to Saudi for crash rescue
48-015	153-38491	RB-45C-1-NA	324th SRS/91st SRW	Shot down 4 Dec 1950 near Yalu River
48-016	153-38492	RB-45C-1-NA	324th SRS/91st SRW	Cr 6 Jun 1952 near Yokota AB Japan
48-017	153-38493	RB-45C-1-NA	As JRB-45C	Preserved-SAC Museum -Offut AFB
48-018	153-38494	RB-45C-1-NA	3200 AMS/3200 AMG	W/o 7 Jul 1951- ground fire
48-019	153-38495	RB-45C-1-NA	19th SRS/ 47th BW	Wfu 1 Aug 1957
48-020	153-38496	RB-45C-1-NA	343rd SRS/ 91st SRG	W/o 12 Sep 1951 on take off
48-021	153-38497	RB-45C-1-NA	323rd SRS/ 91st SRG	W/o 7 Jun 1951 on take off
48-022	153-38498	RB-45C-1-NA	19th SRS/ 47th BW	Wfu Sep 1957
48-023	153-38499	RB-45C-1-NA	19th SRS/ 47th BW	28 Apr 1958- to Turkey for fire use
48-024	153-38500	RB-45C-1-NA	323rd SRS/ 91st SRG	W/o 28 Apr 1951-crash landed due to u/c failure
48-025	153-38501	RB-45C-1-NA	19th SRS/ 47th BW	Withdrawn from use
48-026	153-38502	RB-45C-1-NA	323rd SRS/ 91st SRG	W/o 15 May 1951- landing accident-ground loop
48-027	153-38503	RB-45C-1-NA	323rd SRS/ 91st SRG	Wfu 6 Sep 1957- to RAF for fire service use
48-028	153-38504	RB-45C-1-NA	324th SRS/ 91st SRG	Cr 8 Feb 1951- engine failure
48-029	153-38505	RB-45C-1-NA	19th SRS/ 47th BW	Wfu 6 Sep 1957- to Germany for fireservice use
48-030	153-38506	RB-45C-1-NA	323rd SRS/ 91st SRG	W/o 7 May 1951-engine failure and fire
48-031	153-38507	RB-45C-1-NA	NAA	W/o 4 Apr 1949- crash landed after mech failure
48-032	153-38508	RB-45C-1-NA	324th SRS/ 91st SRG	W/o 4 Aug 1951-landing accident
48-033	153-38509	RB-45C-1-NA	19th SRS/ 47th BW	Withdrawn from use
48-034	153-38510	RB-45C-1-NA	19th SRS/ 47th BW	Wfu 2 Oct 1957- to France for fire service use
48-035	153-38511	RB-45C-1-NA	19th SRS/ 47th BW	Wfu 9 Sep 1957-to Alconbury for fireservice use
48-036	153-38512	RB-45C-1-NA	19th SRS/ 47th BW	Wfu 2 Oct 1957-to France for fire service use
48-037	153-38513	RB-45C-1-NA	AMA	Wfu 17 Dec 1957- Norton AFB
48-038	153-38514	RB-45C-1-NA	19th SRS/ 47th BW	Withdrawn from use
48-039	153-38515	RB-45C-1-NA	19th SRS/ 47th BW	Withdrawn from use
48-040	153-38516	RB-45C-1-NA	324th SRS/ 91st SRG	Wfu 17 Dec 1957- Norton AFB
48-041	153-38517	RB-45C-1-NA	19th SRS/ 47th BW	Wfu 2 Oct 1957- to France for fire service use
48-042	153-38518	RB-45C-1-NA	19th SRS/ 47th BW	Withdrawn from use
48-043	153-38519	RB-45C-1-NA	HQ Sdn 91st SRW	Wfu 26 Sep 1957- to Woodbridge for fire service use

NAA XB-45 prototype 45-59479 not only sports blocked out nose but a sunshade above the pilots position as well. This was not a standard item, it was needed to counter the high temperatures experienced whilst flying from Muroc.

On its way to the final assembly area is the first XB-45 being moved on a low loader. The covers over the nose and engines were there for protection not disguise.

When it was realised that the B-45 fleet was not going to be used in the manner of its WW2 counterparts it was decided that the glazed nose section could be replaced by a solid panel thus reducing the vulnerability of the airframe. B-45A 47-046 was serving with the 47th BW when photographed.

APPENDIX TWO
NAA B-45A/D SOLID NOSE MODIFICATIONS

B-45A-5	47-059
	47-061
47-023	47-062
47-029	47-065
47-030	47-081
47-043	47-082
47-048	47-085
47-050	47-089
47-055	
47-057	B-45C
47-058	48-010

NOTE- this list is constructed using photographic evidence and is therefore incomplete. It is highly likely that most of the aircraft assigned to the 47th Bomb Wing were so modified. Should further information become available the updates will be posted on the website.

Photographed at Muroc is the first XB-45 prototype complete with canopy sunshading. This aircraft was built with the short span tailplane which some instability during flight trials.

The final B-45 prototype, 45-59481, was retained for trials purposes for which purpose it was subject to the various modification programmes applied to the operational fleet.

RB-45C 48-012 is seen here undergo preparation for flight prior to being delivered to USAF. In service the aircraft flew from Alconbury on reconnaissance duties before ending its days as a rescue trainer in France.

Another airframe that would spend its final days in France as a fire and rescue trainer was RB-45C 48-036 seen here sporting the markings of the 19th SRS based at Alconbury.

This overview of B-45C 48-005 reveals many upper surface details including the layout of the engine nacelle anti glare panel plus the different colours of the alloy skin. This aircraft was utilised by Northrop as part of a drone control programme for which purpose it was designated EDB-45C.

APPENDIX THREE
NAA B-45/RB-45 TECHNICAL DETAILS

XB-45

Crew	2 pilot and co-pilot
Wingspan	89ft 6 ins
Fuselage	74ft
Height to top of fin	25 ft 2 ins
Wing area	1,175 sq ft
Basic gross weight	41,876 lbs
Normal operational weight	66,820 lbs
Max gross weight	82,600 lbs
Max range	2,921 miles
Range with 8,350 lbs of bombs	2,236 miles
Range with 14,000 lbs of bombs	1,700 miles

Engines [also installed in B-45A-1]
4x Allison J35-A-7 rated at 4,000 lbs.st

Performance
Maximum speed	483 mph @ 30,000 ft
	516 mph @ 14,000 ft
	494 mph @ sea level
Service ceiling	37,600 ft
Initial climb rate	2,070 ft/min

Two North American Aviation products in formation together, the F-86 Sabre and the B-45 Tornado. Of the two the fighter would gain the greater and long lasting fame.

B-45A-1 A-5 B-45C

Crew ....pilot, co-pilot, bombardier/navigator, tail gunner
Wingspan...89 ft
Wingspan with tip tanks......................................96 ft B-45C only
Fuselage..75 ft 3 ins
Height to top of fin..25 ft 2 ins
Wing area...1,175 sq ft
Basic gross weight..........................45,694 lbs (A) 48,903 lbs (C)
Normal operational weight.. 82,600 lbs
Max gross weight..........................81,418 lbs (A) 112,952 lbs (C)
Max range..2,426 miles (A) (C)
Range with 22,000 lbs bomb..1,000 miles
Combat range with 10,000 lbs bombs......................533 miles (A)
　　　　　　　　　　　　　　　　　　　　　　　1,008 miles (C)

Engines
4x General Electric J47-GE-13/15 rated at 5,200 lbs.st or 4x J79-GE-7/9 or 6,000 lbs with water injection (C)

Performance
Maximum speed....571 mph @ 3,500 ft (A) 579 mph @sea level
　　　　　　　　　503 mph @ 37,000 ft (A) 509 mph @ 32,500 ft
Cruising speed....470 mph @ 35,000 ft (A) 456 mph @ 35,000 ft
Stalling speed...125 mph (A)
　　　　　　　　　　　　　　　　　　　　　　　　　153 mph (C)
Initial climb rate..5,950 ft/min (A)
　　　　　　　　　　　　　　　　　　　　　　　5,800 ft/min (C)
Combat ceiling..42,800 ft
Service ceiling...46,400 ft (A)
　　　　　　　　　　　　　　　　　　　　　　　　　43,200 ft (C)

Armament
2x 0.50 inch M-3 machine guns in tail turret (A) M-7 (C)
Max bomb load................................22,000 lbs Grand Slam bomb
　　　　　　　　　　　or 27x 500 lbs or 2x 4,000 nuclear weapons.

In order to calibrate the airspeed indicators properly extra pitot heads were mounted on the wingtips of the first XB-45. The data gathered would provide comparisons between the primary pitot head and the wingtip so that corrections could be made to the system. Note the national marking lack the red bars introduced when USAF was formed as a seperate service.

45-59480 was the second prototype and bore a similarity to its older sibling although it would feature the enlarged tailplane plus other systems.

RB-45C

Crew	pilot, co-pilot, photo-navigator
Wingspan	89 ft
Wingspan with tip tanks	96 ft
Fuselage	75 ft 9 ins
Height to top of fin	25 ft 2 ins
Wing area	1,175 sq ft
Basic weight	49,984 lbs
Basic gross weight	82,600 lbs
Maximum gross weight	110,721 lbs
Max range	2,530 miles

Engines
4x General Electric J47-GE-13/15 rated at 5,200 lbs.st or 6,000 lbs with water injection or 4x J79-GE-7/9 rated at 5,820 lbs.st with water injection

Performance

Maximum speed	570 mph @ 4,000 ft
Combat speed	506 mph @ 32,700 ft
Stalling speed	153 mph
Initial climb rate	4,340 ft/min
Combat ceiling	40,250 ft
Service ceiling	46,400 ft

Armament 2x0.50 inch M-7 machine guns (when fitted)
25x 188 lbs M-122 photoflash bombs in fwd bomb bay

JATO consisted of two Aerojet XLR13-AJ-1 of 4,000 lbs. thrust each with 60-second duration

Pictured over mountainous terrain is the second XB-45. During many of its test flights the crew was limited to three as the tail gun position was normally unoccupied.

This close up of 45-59480 reveals the marking carried on the upper surface of the aircraft the most obvious of which is the turbine band around the engine nacelles.

One of a handful of survivors B-45C 48-010 is preserved at the National Museum of the USAF where it is resplended in 47th BW marks although it spent much of its life as a test bed.

While the reconnaissance machines were under the command of the 47th BW in the UK this organisations primary aircraft was the B-45A/C. Here 47-087 is shown on display at a USAF open day. The fate of this aircraft was to end its days as a firemans plaything in Spain.

This underview of the XB-45 prototype shows the access panels for the wing tanks amongst others.